The DEVIL
in the
CLASSROOM

The DEVIL in the CLASSROOM

Hostility in American Education

JAMES MARSHALL

Schocken Books · New York

First published by Schocken Books 1985
10 9 8 7 6 5 4 3 2 1   85 86 87 88
Copyright © 1985 by James Marshall

Library of Congress Cataloging in Publication Data
Marshall, James, 1896–
The devil in the classroom.
    1. Teacher-student relationships—United States.
2.Hostility (Psychology)   3. School management and
organization—United States—Psychological aspects.
4. Community and school—United States—Psychological
aspects.   5. School discipline—United States—
Psychological aspects.   I. Title.
LB1033.M257   1985   371.1′02   84–23510

Designed by Nancy Dale Muldoon
Manufactured in the United States of America
ISBN 0–8052–3968–5

To the memory of RENSIS LIKERT and to my grandchildren, great-grandchildren, and theirs ad infinitum

Contents

Foreword

For seventeen years I was a member of the New York City Board of Education, president for four years. There I had the opportunity of watching, and sometimes participating in, the administration of a school system. I was helped by a succession of able young men who were my confidential secretaries for spells of two or three years, and who were trained in administration. I witnessed the differences in the atmosphere of school districts and schools resulting from the style of administration of superintendents and principals. Such differences are often observed but the lessons to be drawn from them are infrequently utilized.

Later I taught human relations and problem solving at the Graduate School of Public Administration at New York University. Almost all of my students held minor administrative positions in government or voluntary organizations and I learned from them too. But I was shocked to discover how these mature people had been trained to depend on the instructor. They waited to be told what texts or references to use, the very pages they should be prepared for at the next session, and the questions they were expected to answer.

For two summers I attended seminars of the National Training Laboratory at Bethel, Maine, and I was for a time on the staff of the Boston University Human Relations Laboratory. There I learned the values of free discussions in which the participants were not dependent on the leader of a group.

Over many years I have visited schools in the United States and foreign schools with as varied cultures as those of Western Europe, the subcontinent of Asia, Indonesia, the Philippines, and East Africa. Although I have a sense of the atmosphere in the schools (high tension in the French lycée and relaxation in Indonesia, for example), I do not feel secure enough in what I believe I witnessed to draw upon those experiences.

In my early days at the bar I was active in civil liberties litigation and in later years I followed court decisions concerning the liberties of teachers and students and their rights vis-à-vis autocratic school boards and administrators.

What I have learned from these experiences, association with social psychologists, and reading I have attempted to elaborate in this book and to bring together some relevant literature on hostility, its effects, and some means to its melioration.

Probably the greatest stimulant to my thinking, or better, to my awareness of the importance of the atmosphere created by the style of leadership, was the study made by Kurt Lewin and his associates, Ronald Lippitt and Ralph White. A group of us at the Board of Education—a couple of board members, some superintendents and principals—used to meet for dinner monthly to discuss educational problems. On one occasion one of our members showed a picture of that research. It involved three groups of youngsters whose leaders acted in a manner that was "autocratic," "democratic," or "laissez-faire." What stood out was the hostility developed in the autocratic and laissez-faire groups compared with the democratic. (The study will be discussed in detail in chapter 1.) To many others this research by Lewin has also been the taking-off point for thought and practice in teaching and administration. However, it has not permeated educational administration or methods to any considerable degree, partly because of the sluggishness and self-defensiveness of bureaucracies, partly because of the common habit of thought that effective administration must be autocratic, and partly because schools of education have not emphasized the lesson of that study.

The first thing I did was to ask George D. Stoddard, at that time the New York State superintendent of schools (Stoddard had been director of the Iowa Child Welfare Research Station where the Lewin experiment had been conducted), to present an account of Lewin's research and findings to the Board of Education and most of our superintendents. His clear presentation lit no spark. The flash that Stoddard, a few superintendents, and I had seen did not, apparently, reach the others. Perhaps they could not recognize that there was autocracy in their schools and that that had relevance to such hostility as existed. I was myself deflated by this failure and stopped there. In doing so I too failed. I failed to realize the inadequacy of the didactic.

At the end of my service on the New York City Board of Education, in a series of articles in the *New York Herald Tribune* (1952), I tried to give an account of my experiences and to state some of the problems that I saw. I wrote:

> . . . The problem in all government is how to reduce hostility or at least how to control or channel it. That seems to me to be one of the basic problems in connection with the pressures brought upon the school system.
>
> Something has been done in recent years to reduce hostility within the system. More could be done through consultation between school personnel on all levels.

Unfortunately, the problem of hostility in education remains too little considered or addressed. This book, I hope, will stimulate serious consideration of hostility in the classroom.

Introduction: The Frame of Reference

What a Stew of Criticism

We like to believe that our schools train our children to be independent but disciplined members of our democratic society. But do we all want this? May we not simultaneously want children who grow up obedient and dependent? We want our children to be able to read and understand what they read, to communicate clearly in writing and by speech, to master the basics of arithmetic, and to understand something of the world they inhabit. We claim to want our schools to be egalitarian. Can we be sure we do?

We are told that American education today is faulty, is inadequate in a number of ways and for a number of causes. Many students leave high school unable to read above a fourth-, sixth-, or eighth-grade level. There is rarely a week in which some book, article, news report, or institution does not scold our schools. They have been called "blackboard jungles," "storage bins." Teachers are said to be indifferent, ignorant, or unskilled. They and their students fail to be motivated. The school day and the school year are too short. Kindergarten and first grade should begin at a younger age. Mediocrity! The "rising tide of mediocrity." And we have contradictions: educational funds are said to be wasted; on the other hand larger school budgets are declared necessary. We must get good teachers and we want them to remain in their professions, but we cannot pay them enough.

What a stew of criticism there is. Curriculum is not sufficiently centered. There is a cry for concentration on fundamentals, basics (variously defined), and for the abandonment of "nonessential" subjects. School-team sports tend to be regarded to be essential. Foreign languages and the arts are claimed by some to be necessary and by others to be costly frills that interfere with fundamentals. Science usually takes second place. Parents are criticized for not taking enough interest in their children's schooling; but when they do show signs of interest and concern, they are felt to be interfering. Schools are solemnly directed to place greater emphasis on morals and ethics but are discouraged from being critical of officials, our economic system, and, especially, of teachers and what and how they teach.

Then there is that well-regarded leader in education, Diane Ravitch (1983), who would take us back fifty years to the creed of Hutchins, Adler, and Van Doren, et al., who themselves based the curricula they advocated on the seven liberal arts of the medieval universities.

The one thing apparent is that the way we educate our children has failed to meet the expectations or the desires of very nearly everyone.

The year 1983 was a year in which the quality of American education was front-page news. A library shelf of reviews and criticisms of American education was published.* Most of the

---

*For example: *A Nation at Risk: The Imperative for Educational Reform,* National Commission on Excellence in Education, 1983; *High School: A Report on Secondary Education in America,* The Carnegie Foundation for the Advancement of Teaching, Ernest L. Boyer (Harper & Row, 1983); "The Arts and Humanities in America's Schools," *Daedalus,* Summer 1983; *A Place Called School: Prospects for the Future,* John I. Goodlad (McGraw-Hill, 1983); *The Troubled Crusade: American Education, 1945–1980,* Diane Ravitch (Basic Books, 1983); and in 1984 " 'Getting Tough' in the Schools—A Critique of the Conservative Prescription," Deborah Meier, *Dissent,* Winter 1984; *Horace's Compromise: The Dilemma of the American High School,* Theodore R. Sizer (Houghton Mifflin, 1984).

emphases and recommendations have been on such things as time spent in class, teachers' salaries, the form of the curriculum. Except for the Carnegie Report, the Goodlad and Sizer studies, there was little consideration of teachers and students as persons. None of the proposals considered hostility as a phenomenon of schools. A Nation at Risk proposes as one of its chief remedies a longer school day and a longer school year. Ernest L. Boyer, the principal author of the Carnegie Foundation Report, commented, "The issue is not more time but better use of what we have." (The New York Times, September 16, 1983)

If one considers the hostility now existing in schools, a lengthening of the day and year can only be punitive. How can one attain higher quality by making students and teachers work longer in an environment and with a process they dislike, one that is already jammed with hostility? When present teaching methods and school administration are largely autocratic in nature and result in much resistance to learning and a sense of humiliation on the part of teachers and students, will more time produce more learning or more hostile counterattack?

Certainly a curriculum can be strengthened. The mastery of English, written and spoken, ought to be a "central curriculum objective." Mathematics, science, foreign languages ought to be included in a curriculum to create educated citizens. The curriculum, loosened in the 1960s to satisfy the demand of young people for freedom from discipline and for greater choice, became mushy and scattered.

Granted the need for better educational experience in written English. This would require a consideration of class size, which is absent. In a large class there can be less feedback. Possibly a teacher in the lower elementary grades with classes of under thirty could read and correct children's papers and give them feedback. But what about high-school teachers who may have several classes of forty students who would be expected to write longer papers than children in the early grades? Here are difficulties presented that are not considered by the reports (except for Sizer). While more written English with feedback can be required, achievement of the goal of the Carnegie Report is doubtful until such time as computers can correct papers and read a multitude of handwritings.

There are recommendations made for more homework. It is pointed out that homework is emphasized in the more effective schools. Homework certainly can increase the depth of learning.

However, even where homework is required it may be extremely difficult, if not impossible, in a poverty area for children to find a quiet place to do their homework. Space may be missing in their homes. Encouragement by parents (or a parent) may be lacking. Competition with the TV programs played by other members of the family may be defeating.

The attention these 1983 reports give to education is wholesome. It can be stimulating, but the reports will not solve or substantially improve schooling without attention to school atmosphere, the problems children bring to school, their and their teachers' needs for a sense of social power—as well as the financial implications of even the best suggestions.

Frame of Reference

Teachers, students of education, the public—indeed, almost all of us—have tended to address the failure of schools to teach children "basics" from the point of view of traditional education. Our criticisms have related to teacher training, curricula, methods of teaching, class size, promotion programs, reading scores, and other tools of evaluation. Without denying relevance to such criticisms, may one not question their importance by shifting the frame of reference? There is danger in looking even questioningly at problems from a single point of view, especially when that point of view is traditional, that is, habitual with us. The casts and situations in a school system and every classroom always change. Limiting evaluations and a search for solutions to one frame of reference may limit the possibility to discover solutions.

A shift in the frame of reference may reveal the nature of a problem to be quite different. The Likerts (1976) give an entertaining example: In a class in problem solving for engineering students at New York University, a professor asked the class to think of the numbers 2, 4, 6, and 8, and then to tell him the next two numbers. They responded 10 and 12. Then he asked them to think of the numbers 1, 2, 4, and 8, and tell him the next two numbers. The class immediately said 16 and 32. Finally, the professor asked them to think of the numbers 14, 34, 42, 72, 96, and 110, and tell him the next two numbers. The students, conceiving this to be another mathematical problem, worked on it for several weeks without any solution. The class agreed that their assumptions were that this was a mathematical problem. In fact, the professor explained: "The problem is not a number series. Another assumption or frame of reference is needed because the next two numbers are 116 and 125. These numbers are the express station stops on the 7th Avenue subway," in New York City. It was not a knowledge of the New York subway system that was important but a recognition that one frame of reference could not be used to resolve different problems.

The frame of reference of this book will shift from the more traditional analyses of what's wrong with our schools (some of which have been mentioned) to teacher-student, supervisor-teacher, and community interaction and to the resulting hostility in classrooms that impedes healthy relationships and distorts the process of learning. In this framework it may be possible to find causes and remedies that may evade us by traditional analyses.

Parents and children, teachers, and supervisors, all of us, live and work in an environment that involves personal relations. These contribute to the sense of having or losing social power at each level and between each level from the kindergarten child to the school board member. *There is nothing more basic in education than developing and maintaining environments attentive to those behaviors that contribute to the sense of social power, if resistance to learning and avoidance of hostility are to be kept to a minimum.* After that the traditional subject-matter basics will be easier to achieve. Otherwise the cry for more emphasis on basics, fundamentals, a longer school year or a longer school day will be only more modes of the moment, other transient cure-alls.

One does not customarily look to the Supreme Court for a statement of educational policy but the following strong statement is fundamental:

> Scholarship cannot flourish in an atmosphere of suspicion and distrust. Teachers and students must always remain free to inquire, to study and to evaluate, to gain new maturity and understanding; otherwise our civilization will stagnate and die." (Sweezy v. New Hampshire 1957)

This neatly enunciates the point that relationships of trust and freedom are necessary for students and teachers "to gain maturity and understanding."

Within the frame of reference of this book we face a number of salient questions. To what extent do autocracy and resultant hostility in the educational hierarchy and the interaction among the various levels of hierarchy affect teaching? In other words, what are the effects of the common administrative interactions upward and downward on the classroom as a "marketplace of ideas"? Does the prevailing school atmosphere train future leaders of our nation "through wide exposure to that robust exchange of ideas which discovers truth 'out of a multitude of tongues, [rather] than through any kind of authoritative selection' "? [Keyishian v. Board of Regents of U. of St. of N.Y. 1967]

The classroom as a "marketplace for ideas" is critical to an intelligent, participative democracy. The questions are: how can administration be modeled so that both teachers and students will be free to inquire and evaluate, to have greater space for independent thought and communication? To what degree is hostility an impediment and to what extent can this impediment be reduced?

The DEVIL
in the
CLASSROOM

1 Autocracy and Hostility

Raising kids is part joy and part guerrilla warfare.
—Asner, Raised in Anger

William James has compared the classroom with a battlefield in which the opposing forces are the teacher who tries for discipline and to achieve adult standards and the pupils who strive for the interests of their own age group. (James 1899) So the classroom may be considered as a battlefield to achieve growth with an ever-present threat of diminishment. (The diminishment of students and teachers and resulting hostility will be discussed in chapters which follow.)

Each generation has its own subculture. Each tends to resist the other and hostility may be generated, especially if one tends to denigrate the other and give a sense of lack of esteem, the older for the younger or the younger for the older. This is well described by Aristophanes in "The Clouds" (1942).

> I told him to go and fetch his harp and help the supper
>   along
> By singing us good Simonides' Ram or another fine song.
> But he replied that to sing at meals was coarse and quite
>   out of style,

And Simonides now was obsolete—had been for a good
   long while.
I really could hardly restrain myself at his finicking,
   poppy-cock ways,
But I did and I asked him to give us then a selection from
   AEschylus' plays.
But he answered, "AEschylus is to me an unmitigated
   bore,
A turgid, swollen-up, wind-bag thing that does nothing
   but ramp and roar."
When he talked like that my bosom began to heave
   extremely fast,
But I kept myself in and politely said, "Then give us one of
   the last,
Of the very newest you young men like." And he started a
   shameful thing
Euripides wrote, the sort of stuff no gentlemen ever would
   sing,
Then, then, I could bear no more. I confess, I stormed and
   struck him too,
And he turned on me, his own father, he did, and beat me
   black and blue.

Son

And rightly too when you dared to blame that wisest of
   poets—he
Who is high over all, Euripides.

Father

The boy's just a fool, I see.

Out of the classroom situation and the interactions of generations, it is easy to trigger hostility.

Hostility

Let us pause here to define the meaning of hostility as
used in this book.

Hostility is a tendency of an organism to do harm to another
organism or itself, generally leading to harmful aggression, although the hostility and aggression may be repressed and the
harm is then done to the unconscious self. Hostility and aggressive behavior are reactions by the organism to imbalance, are

means to reestablish equilibrium, or stability. Together they constitute counterattacks when a sense of power—especially social power or self-esteem—is reduced or felt to be threatened.

Hostility has a broad band. It may be expressed along a continuum extending from gossip, spreading rumors and slander, to deprivations, punitiveness, and various exercises of force or violence against property or persons. Anger, expressed or repressed, is a symptom of hostility. In a sense hostility is a feeling that induces aggressiveness, that is, the "[t]endency to attack or injure, or to push one's own interests or ideas forward, or to carry out one's plans despite opposition." (Murphy 1947)

The classroom battlefield may bristle with hostility not only because teacher and pupil may have different goals. Attack and counterattack, rarely perceived and more rarely verbalized, may be aroused because of different experiences and subcultures that have colored the perceptions and values of each generation (as in the case of Aristophanes' father and son) and because of what power structure in the educational heirarchy does to the sense of social power of teacher and pupil.

Defensive and Aggressive Hostility

Man is the only creature engaging in malignant aggression, ready to kill his own species or destroy his own or others' artifacts, not solely in defense. (Fromm 1973) However, it is not always easy to tell what behavior of a child (or teacher) is defensive, what malignant. Promptly labeling behavior as malignant avoids the necessity to look more deeply into the facts, to search for some empirical evidence, to learn what is motivating the behavior. Essentially it comes to the very personal questions for the teacher: "How much student behavior is a hostile reaction to something I have said or done? How can I modify my behavior?" Or it may be: "What has the class done to stimulate a hostile self-defensive response and how can I get the class to see what its behavior has set in motion?" Only after that is it proper to look outside the classroom for causes. Teachers like others will tend to block out their own responsibility and look abroad to explain the hostility of others.

Aggression can be directed at the "responsible" person who arouses hostility; or there may be displaced aggression through blind, random actions, to smash anything in sight. School windows may be broken, someone's property may be destroyed or injured or gossip may be spread, gossip not mentioning the person attacked but an associate or subordinate. These are some examples of displaced aggression. The current prevalence of graffiti is an example, too, of random aggression (a hostile use of primitive art?) to enhance ego and achieve a sense of power balance.

Whether it is aroused by the teacher, or the school pattern, or some other power-reducing instrument, aggression may be an expression of revenge. For " '[R]evenge is essentially rooted in the feeling of power and superiority. It arises consequent on the experience of injury, and its aim is to enhance the self-feeling, which has been lowered or degraded by the injury suffered.' " (Westermarck 1932) Revenge is most satisfactory for this purpose if it can be directed against the aggressor but this is not essential. In any event, revenge, whether direct or indirect, is an attempt to reestablish a balance of power.

However, all hostilely induced reactions are not negative. Anger may reverberate with an inner trumpet call to overcome obstacles. Sometimes a student may put in extra effort to prove the obstructionist, the depreciator, the person who reduces a sense of power to be wrong. A teacher may persist and show better results by the use of unconventional methods. A silent alliance may be formed between teachers and students against a hostile administration.

Lewin's Classical Experiment

For those who are not acquainted with the Lewin, Lippitt, and White study (1939), and to refresh the memory of others, a summary of the experiment may be helpful. Three kinds of play groups were established, each under a different kind of leadership: autocratic, democratic, and laissez-faire. Each group was subjected to the three kinds of leadership and each leader assumed the three leadership roles with different groups. That is, each child and each leader participated in each experience with the three styles of leadership. The children were about eleven years old and met in their groups after school.

In the autocratic situation the leader was not unfriendly but would tell the group what to do and how to do it and would make all judgments as to progress. In the democratic group the style, goals, and means of reaching them were determined by the members of the group including the leader. In the laissez-faire situation the leader only answered questions and made no suggestions.

Definite hostility was expressed 186 times in the autocratic group and in the democratic group only 6 times. This represented 18 percent of all recorded social interactions in the autocratic groups but less than 1 percent in the democratic groups. There were aggressive demands for attention 39 times in the autocratic and only 3 times in the democratic. At the end of the sessions there was considerable destruction of their own property by the boys in the autocratic groups. This did not occur at all in the democratic groups. There was scapegoating in one case and several boys dropped out during the autocratic club periods.

While most of the children in the autocratic group expressed hostility, there were a considerable number who were submissive. Submissive actions toward the leader occurred 256 times in the autocratic situation and 134 in the democratic. In the autocratic group remarks to the leader that were dependent averaged 14 by each of the boys who reacted aggressively, 16 by the boys who reacted submissively, 4 in laissez-faire and 6 in democratic groups. Thus, there was not only greater hostility but also greater dependence on authority where leadership was autocratic. (The laissez-faire situation will be more fully considered in the next chapter.)

When the boys were transferred from a group with one kind of leadership to another with a different kind of leadership their behavior changed too. When the change was from a democratic to an autocratic group leader "the group that had formerly been friendly, cooperative and full of life, became within a short half hour a rather apathetic-looking gathering without initiative." When the transitions were made from the autocratic to a freer democratic atmosphere, on several occasions those who had been submissive exhibited aggressive behavior. After "the thrill of a new-found freedom apparently wore off," it took time to adapt to democracy following the autocratic experience. (Cartwright 1959, 1966) "The change from autocracy to democracy," Lewin said, "seemed to take somewhat more time than that from democracy to autocracy. Autocracy is imposed on the individual. Democracy he has to learn." (Marrow 1969)

One of the outstanding observations of the researchers was the difference in initiative and interest between those youngsters in the autocratic group and those in the democratic group. When the leader in the former left the room, work stopped. In the latter case, work continued as it had during the presence of the leader.

Replications of the Lewin, Lippitt, White experiment in Japan produced similar results, although "the American children showed more direct aggressive behavior than ours [Japanese]." (Misumi 1973) This meant to the experimenters that the sociocultural aspects of group behavior were not as strong as the situational. That is, although there were differences in national cultures the effects of different kinds of leadership were similar.

While Lewin, Lippitt, and White were conducting their classic experiment on the effect of three climates of leadership (authoritarian, laissez-faire, and democratic) in Iowa, Charles H. Judd of the University of Chicago, a leading professor of education in the country at the time, visited one of the experimental groups. Judd remarked to Lewin, "Professor Lewin, this class is the most accurate representation of the typical American schoolroom I have ever seen." Lewin was embarrassed and replied, "But, Dr. Judd, you have been observing our rendition of an *authoritarian* situation." (Stoddard 1961)

Hostility in the Schoolroom

The regimentation of our schools and the imposition of curricula on students generally regardless of the questions they want answered contribute to the conflict. This phenomenon is well stated by Cantor, one of the most original minds in American education:

> The American school system is one of the most regimented social structures in American life. School program is laid down by adult boards who administer the school system. Relatively little choice is allowed students in the selection of subject-matter or activities. The way to learn, when to learn, what to learn, how much to learn and how to treat that learning, are generally standardized." (Cantor 1956)

In a recent study in England, Rutter et al. (1979) found that "[p]upils in high delinquency schools perceived the teachers as more authoritarian and the schools as less committed to learning" than in schools with less delinquency. This was so for both delinquent and nondelinquent pupils in the schools.

Compulsory education results in tension, as all compulsion does, and as formal education often counters the subculture of youth this tension becomes aggravated. With a warning that tensions and conflicts are not equally intense in all schools, Rutter and his associates in their study of English schools say:

> . . . Schooling is compulsory and the very fact that children *have* to attend is likely to make for tensions and antagonism. Thus, many years ago Waller (1932) wrote, "Teacher and pupil confront each other with attitudes from which the underlying hostility can never be altogether removed." Gordon (1957) in his study of one American high school noted the force of the informal student subculture which stood in opposition to the official educational ideology. (Rutter, et al. 1979)

Augustine in his *Confessions* reported a conflicting pattern of values, which is in essence what William James referred to as a battlefield. He wrote:

> ... [W]hat miseries and mockeries did I then experi-
> ence, when obedience to my teachers was set before me as
> proper to my boyhood, that I might flourish in this world,
> and distinguish myself in the science of speech, which
> should get me honor amongst men, and deceitful riches!
> After that I was put to school to get learning of which I
> (worthless as I was) knew not what use there was; and yet,
> if slow to learn, I was flogged! (Augustine 1943)

He said that he and his comrades were not in want of memory or capacity

> [B]ut we delighted only in play; and we were punished
> for this by those who were doing the same things them-
> selves. But the idleness of our elders they call business,
> whilst boys who do the like are punished by those same
> elders, and yet neither boys nor men find any pity. For will
> any one of good sense approve of my being whipped be-
> cause, as a boy, I played ball, and so was hindered from
> learning quickly those lessons by means of which, as a
> man, I should play more unbecomingly?

He recalled, too, that the very teacher who beat him was, when defeated in some little argument with a coteacher, "more tor-mented by anger and envy than I when beaten by a playfellow in a match at ball."

Why Should Autocratic Behavior Elicit Hostile Responses?

Murray Horwitz (1956) suggests that when a person's sense of social power is reduced, hostility is expressed as a counterattack to reestablish his or her sense of power, to achieve a new equilibrium. In his experiment Horwitz found that a teacher who reduces his or her students' sense of power and, therefore, self-esteem stimulates a need in the students to counterattack. He reports that the strength of this need varied directly with the degree of the students' sense of reduction of the power they expected within the social environment, here, the classroom. The degree of hostile counterattack was a direct index of the degree of reduction of the students' expected sense of social power. The hostility expressed was higher where power restoration did not occur, when it was not permitted by the authority or was suppressed or repressed by the student, than where it was fully restored. Expression of hostility may well be a cue to teachers that they have been deemed autocratic by their students.

Hostility directed toward a teacher may be displacement of hostility derived from home or community conditions that reduce the student's sense of his or her social power; or, as Gurr (1970) puts it, he or she may rebel against a sense of deprivation relative to others. This is illustrative of the basic frustration-aggression theory that the greater the frustration the greater will be the aggression against the source of the frustration.

What is generally overlooked is that a pervasive element in our schools (and American schools are not unique in this) is their autocratic, undemocratic nature, from classroom to top administration. Autocracy may arouse hostility or subservience. The one is disruptive, the other deadening. Both tend to block the realization of capacities to learn and teach, to inquire and create. Furthermore, autocracy contradicts the basic values we purport to teach: freedom, democracy, independence, and self-discipline, and, therefore, they may not be learned in school. Is this, perhaps, because we do not want or trust children who are free, democratic, independent, or self-disciplined?

The nurture and results of hostility are rarely put in perspective. Instead of thinking in terms of the results of autocracy and hostility, the public generally cries out for more discipline (law and order) and less laissez-faire (permissiveness) in the schools. But the by-products of more discipline may be at best as destructive of personal growth as permissiveness. One of these by-products may be counterattack, hostility, and aggressiveness.

As far as aggression is *biologically* given in man's genes,
it is not spontaneous, but a defense against threats to man's
vital interests, that of his growth and his and the species'
survival. (Fromm 1973)

Discontent is not a function of the difference between what
people want and what they have, but rather between what they
want and believe they are capable of achieving. (Gurr 1970)
Children may want good marks. They will be particularly
angered by a low grade if they believe themselves capable of a
better one, especially if some other children are thought to get a
better one undeservedly.

Gurr gives several examples. People "may be subjectively deprived with reference to their expectations even though an objective observer might not judge them to be in want. Similarly,
the existence of what the observer judges to be abject poverty or
'absolute deprivation' is not necessarily thought to be unjust or
irremediable by those who experience it." He also suggests that a
student may believe that upon completion of school he or she is
close to his or her goals, such as status, earning power, or political participation. This, of course, is a common belief. If, on the
other hand, a student finds on graduation that jobs are scarce,
pay is not what he or she expected, his or her family is hostile or
parasitic, and his or her political powers are low, "disillusionment and anger are likely consequences."

People tend to act in accordance with what they believe, to
behave in such a manner as may help them realize their values
or achieve need-satisfaction. They tend to perceive and adjust
the facts and their values so as to justify what they do. (Festinger 1957; Brehm and Cohen 1962) Will they then admit that
their behavior was hostile or, instead, modify belief so as to
justify to themselves what they have done? Will a person tend
to define or redefine hostility, for example, in such a way,
probably unwittingly, so as to justify to himself or herself that
no principle or value has been violated or compromised and
demonstrate to others that he or she has not done wrong? How a
perpetrator of a hostile act (or one who identifies with him or

her) describes the act will probably be quite different from the terms in which a subject of hostility (or those who identify with him or her) will define it.

Defensive Definition

A study by Blumenthal and her associates (1972) of how American men define violence (one form of hostile expression) may be a model of how people define various forms of hostility so as to organize their definitions (perceptions) of facts to accord with their values and interests and avoid guilt feelings.

An interesting finding of the study how different populations of subjects of the research defined violence was that in one population 12 percent of the men questioned in the research did not think looting to be violence, 30 percent did not believe burglary to be violence; in another 30 percent did not see beating students to be violence, and 57 percent did not believe police shooting looters to be violence.

No one cares to consider himself or herself as being "bad." Generally if one advocates, or supports others, in violence, an attempt will be made to justify that violence in order to avoid the feeling of being "bad." "It is easier simply not to recognize actions as immoral, and in the present case recognition can be avoided simply by not classifying acts of violence as 'violence.' " Consequently, those who "identify" strongly with the police and supported high levels of force by police did not define beating students or shooting looters to be violent. The same people would tend to consider behavior of students and black protesters and dissenters, as being violent. Others could not see looting or burglary to be violence. "One would expect therefore that what acts a person calls violence will be related to the kinds of identifications he holds." (Blumenthal et al. 1972)

The groups subject to the research were college students, people who hold college or higher degrees, white union members, whites who "spontaneously mentioned fears of being discriminated against by blacks," and blacks. Only 4 percent of college students and 15 percent of blacks defined sit-ins to be violence. However, 40 percent of the whites spontaneously mentioning fear of being discriminated against by blacks called sit-ins violence, and 59 percent of blacks defined police-shooting looters to be violence, whereas only 23 percent of white union members did.

Blacks more than other groups appeared to see police actions that led to injury as being violent. More than the general population, college students and college-educated men defined such acts as violence, but less often than blacks did.

Draft-card burning, sit-ins, and student protests, which involved dissent but no destructive force, were described as violent by many American men. College students and those with college degrees, however, were less likely to call them violent, blacks less likely to do so than American men in general, and considerably less than white union members or whites who feared reverse discrimination. Curiously, although property damage such as looting and burglary was considered violence generally, college students and those with college degrees "were somewhat less apt to do so than were others."

Similarly, what appears to a teacher to be disrespectful or disorderly conduct by a student may be defined as hostile by the teacher; but the student would probably not define it so. The student may find a teacher's reprimand as hostile but the teacher may believe it necessary to maintain discipline. The definition, then, would be subjective and self-serving. Definition may be a symbol, and as such a means to avoid feeling in the wrong, and a rationalization to justify an attack and put the object of the hostility, the person with different goals and values, in the role of an accused.

Not only do we perceive the facts of a situation in such a way as to make them acceptable but we may let some prior experience mediate an unacceptable situation to make it more comfortable for us. This is illustrated by the story of a young lady in the first grade who was asked to play the part of the innkeeper in a Christmas play about the arrival of Joseph and Mary in Bethlehem. She wept and refused to play such a "cruel" part.

Finally she was induced to accept the role and on the great day of the performance, with her parents and schoolmates present, she came upon the stage and said in a weepy voice, "I'm sorry there's no room for the night, but won't you come in and have a cocktail?"

Insofar as hostility is stimulated by authority, or is a response to a feeling of unfairness in the use of power, it cannot be separated from power and feelings of impotence before power. Power exists to the extent that one person (P) may get another (O) to do something which that other (O) would not otherwise do or to refrain from doing what he would care or tend to do. The extent of the power of P over O is always limited by the resistance of O to the attempted use of power and by the setting in which the power is exercised. Authority, power, is never exercised in a vacuum but in a field that has limits and is encumbered by sources of resistance. For example, peer group solidarity may resist a teacher's efforts to establish classroom norms unacceptable to the students.

Some Teasing Experience

One cannot help but be teased by evidence that young people with a high delinquency rate tend to be less delinquent after they have left school than before. The Vera Institute of Justice (Strasburg 1978) has found that delinquents who left school had higher "police contact rates" while they were in school than did students who remained in school. However, after they had left school their contact rates declined sharply. The students who continued in school, however, had increases in their police contacts.

> The association between dropping out and reduced delinquency was especially strong with regard to delinquents who had been serious offenders: their involvement with serious offenses declined sharply after leaving school.

This, said the report, could not be explained by "class, sex, 'differential visibility,' 'or the deterrent effect of adjudication.' "

The Vera Institute suggests that employment—the earning of money—and marriage effect the lowering of delinquency.

Income is an important need, especially for older adolescents. Property crimes are the most frequent form of delinquent activity: "[S]tatistics indicate that delinquents who pass the age at which leaving school is permitted, and thus become eligible to get jobs, show a significant decline in property offenses."

The Vera Institute report cites Elliot and Voss (1974) who found postschool marriage to be "a more significant deterrent to delinquency than postschool employment."

And then there are those high-school failures who do well in so-called street academies or storefront schools, many of them able to enter college. The common variable in both instances is that these young people are no longer under legal compulsion, subjected to autocratic authority. (Carnegie Quarterly 1968) "[T]he atmosphere is markedly freer and more lively than that in the usual school." The basic rules were drawn by students. The faculty had faith the young people could succeed. Most did.

Nothing can make the point better than the fact that when, because of inability to raise adequate private funds, one of these academies could no longer remain independent and it was taken over by the New York public school system, it became like any other school in its treatment of students.

Deprivation and Hostility

When *aspirations* are unrealized the effect will be feelings of disappointment. Unrealized *expectations*, however, will result in feelings of deprivation. We can tolerate disappointment, as when we go to a store and find that what we wanted to purchase is not in stock or costs far more than what we expected. Deprivation, however, may be intolerable, as when it is felt that one has the right to something and that something is believed to have been denied unfairly. When some object or privilege (often deemed a right) is taken away, a person deprived will often feel impelled to seek some remedy by whatever means he or she may have. Sometimes there is no direct response available and hostility becomes internalized and erupts in some other, perhaps irrelevant situation.

We may not miss or feel deprived if we have never experienced a right or privilege but take one away and we may react with wrath. This is shown in an experiment by Barker, Dembo, and Lewin (1941) who studied frustration of children two to six years old in a play situation. In the first phase of the experiment the children were permitted to play in free, minimally structured activities which allowed imaginative and constructive play. Some of the children used toy telephones and purported to conduct conversations over them. Others drew pictures. After thirty minutes the experimenter lifted a wire-mesh screen in the middle of the room. In the newly opened section were a number of new, attractive, and exciting toys with which the children were encouraged to play. They became absorbed and fascinated. After they had become deeply engaged the experimenter interrupted the play. The children were led to the "old" section of the room and the experimenter then lowered the wire partition, fastening it with a padlock. The "new" toys were fully visible to the children but were now inaccessible.

Two kinds of behavior on the part of the children occurred. The first related to the accessible goals, playing with the conventional toys; and the second to inaccessible goals, the toys beyond the barrier. After the screen had been lowered and locked, children spent an average of one-third of their time trying to penetrate the barrier or escape from the room. Play with the old toys was different from what it had been. Those who had been holding conversations over the telephone began pounding the receivers against a table. Those who had been drawing began to scribble. The higher the level of frustration the less time was given to constructive play. Children of four and a half years, for example, tended toward the behavior of three-year-olds. There was less smiling and singing, more thumbsucking, noisiness, and restless behavior than before they had been permitted to play with the "new" toys. Aggressiveness increased. Some children hit, kicked, and broke objects. There was a 30 percent rise in the number of hostile actions toward the experimenter, and friendly approaches to him were reduced 34 percent. "The amounts of increase in negative emotionality were positively related to strength of frustration." (Marrow 1969) The behavior of the experimenter here was obviously autocratic. The results were hostile and retrogressive.

The field in which action takes place also limits students. The power of the authority looms over them and may force them to violate their values to avoid some penalty. The author, as a small boy, cracked a rather sorry joke that appealed to his classmates who interrupted the lesson with laughter. He was forced by the principal to apologize to the teacher and state that he did not mean to disrupt the class by the laughter of his classmates. This lying, required by the principal to avoid suspension, aroused a sense of guilt and a long hostility toward the school authorities.

Among the many exercises of power that arouse hostility none is more prevalent and disruptive than disrespect. As Plutarch wrote: "Men are usually more stung and galled by reproachful words than hostile actions." (In school bureaucracies teachers, as well as students, may be as humiliated by reproachful words. The vulnerability of teachers will be considered later.)

Although German schools have always been more autocratic than American (the distance between student and teacher generally has been greater there than here), nevertheless we can find similarities in many of our schools to Einstein's experience in a German *Gymnasium*. Einstein was dropped from his *Gymnasium* in Munich because the school felt his attitude to be negative and to have caused other students to be disrespectful toward their teachers. He applied for admittance to the Polytechnic Institute in Zurich and failed to pass the entrance examinations in mathematics. When finally admitted he did not do well. In an autobiographical note he said:

> The hitch in this was, of course, the fact that one had to cram all this stuff into one's mind for the examinations,

whether one liked it or not. This coercion had such a deterring effect [upon] me that, after I had passed the final examination, I found the consideration of any scientific
problems distasteful for me for an entire year. . . . It is, in
fact, nothing short of a miracle that the modern methods of
instruction have not yet entirely strangled the holy curiosity of inquiry; for this delicate little plant, aside from
stimulation, stands mainly in need of freedom; without
this it goes to wreck [sic] and ruin without fail. (Bernstein
1966)

In sum, then, the essentially autocratic nature of our schools
develops more hostility than a more democratic (or participatory) form. Such hostility occurs because of a reduction in a
student's sense of social power, as well as some deprivation,
which also induces hostility. This may be expressed in the
form of counterattack, or sometimes retrogression, or submission. Whether the pattern of leadership be autocratic or democratic the participants will seek a sense of their own power. The
means to achieve it will differ. So also will the results of the
means used.

2 The Myth of Permissiveness: Standards

There has been considerable complaint about permissiveness and lack of discipline in our American schools. Discipline is often equated with punishment. This need not be so. The former contributes to stability, the latter to hostility.

As the quotation from Cantor in chapter 1 illustrates, permissiveness in education has never been complete. No society has been permissive. There are always some customs, some taboos, some sanctions.

It is true that to a certain extent there has been a slackening of discipline, but the permissiveness of our schools is a myth. For example, the organization of the curriculum limits the inquisitiveness of children and the intellectual and social space in which they may move. Schools—and parents too—still punish children who violate adult norms of proper behavior.

The best known example of a permissive society was that in the Garden of Eden. Adam and Eve could do or refrain from doing as they pleased. *They were free except* for one edict, the violation of which caused their expulsion. Yes they were free, but only so far as Authority permitted them to be. It is fascinating that the one prohibition was curiosity, to attempt to partake of forbidden knowledge.

What has been called permissiveness in our schools in fact has been a depreciation of standards. Children have been promoted in spite of failure year after year, requirements for basic knowledge and skills have sometimes been reduced to meaninglessness. In high school there have been so many choices of courses offered to students that sequences in a given subject have frequently been discouraged and learning in the subject has been reduced to a smattering. High-school diplomas are frequently awarded for years served rather than for educational accomplishments. These are all evidence of lack of discipline and lack of standards. But these are not equivalent to permissiveness (see chapter 6).

Diluted standards and enfeebled discipline have come about in our schools for a number of reasons. First, in many city school systems there is a very valid anxiety and fear of violence that teachers often suffer if they apply discipline or punishment to some students, and there is a collateral fear of parental complaint if discipline or punishment is applied even in the form of low marks. There have been cases in which low marks to a black child have resulted in accusations of race discrimination. While anxiety of teachers is understandable it can be minimized, as will be discussed later, if goals are set that are comprehensible and acceptable to teachers and students. Second, in the last generation or so there has been a wider acceptance of variations from norm than by earlier generations. On the whole, American parents have abandoned strict practices of child rearing, sexual relations between adults have been less forbidden and forbidding, and examples of sexual behavior have been set on the screen and television, and by the press. Following the McCarthy era, tolerance of the views of others, that is allowing and respecting other's beliefs and behaviors, became more common among Americans. Finally, to the extent that standards have been relaxed this is also the result of too facile misinterpretations of philosophies concerning children.

Theoretical and Cultural Background of Permissiveness

In the 1920s the theories of Freud assumed an important place in the thinking of Americans. "In many respects," Lionel Trilling writes, "Freud's ideas have established themselves very firmly in our culture. . . . They have had a decisive influence upon our theories of education and of child rearing. . . . We may say that they have become an integral part of our modern intellectual apparatus." (Trilling 1955) They are in the thinking of our age though the source of the ideas may be unrecognized.

More specifically in the field of education John Dewey had already, at the beginning of the century, advocated the downgrading of didactic teaching as an instrument of authority and taught that education was best accomplished by "learning through doing." A little later, since World War II, millions of copies of Dr. Spock's *The Common Sense Book of Baby and Child Care* (1945) have given impetus to what Freud and Dewey taught by instructing parents in many lands and languages, but especially in the United States, in "flexible attitudes" in child rearing.

We have a capacity to live by conveniently distorted notions. Freud's emphasis on man as a biological being freed us from the idea that we were predominantly controlled by our environment. But we also proceeded to misinterpret Freud. As Trilling said, "How easily they [Freud's ideas] are misunderstood—how *strategically* they are misunderstood." Freud's findings that neuroses arise from the repression of sex were "strategically" and wishfully transformed to a post-Victorian dogma that to answer the call of sex, to seek out sexual expression at all (unfaced) costs, was the avenue to mental health, would develop a sound ego, and be an escape from the domination of the superego. (Erikson 1963) By such irrationalizations we disrupted the balance between superego, ego, and id, and gave our young people a weapon in rebellion against their parents and disrupted their own egos, their sense of self-esteem.

For self-esteem is not to be gained by destroying continuity, which is one phase of superego influence, and placing emphasis on the id, that is "doing your own (biological) thing" regardless. In Freudian terms the ego cannot maintain balance when the superego is denied, any more than when the id is denied. The absence of externalized discipline is as threatening to homeostasis, to balance, as is the absence of instinctual expression (neither of course is possible in a pure form). It is always a balance between external sanctions and freedom of instinctual expression that builds a healthy ego, a sense of self-esteem, of social power, of internalized self-discipline and conscience.

The movement, particularly in elementary education, for what has been variously called "the new methods of education," "progressive education," and "the child-centered school" (and sometimes called "the child-dominated school") was stimulated by the teachings of John Dewey. His disciples spread his doctrines and trained hundreds of thousands of teachers and school administrators in his theories of democratic education and the development of the child as a unique personality to be adjusted to a democratic culture. But the democracy which Dewey taught had its own discipline, though the emphasis was on self-discipline rather than on external or authoritarian discipline. It had nothing in common with undisciplined, irresponsible laissez-faire attitudes. To Dewey "The doctrine of *laissez-faire* . . . applied to intelligence" was unsound. To him it went counter to scientific method, which "is as much opposed to go-as-you-please in intellectual matters as it is to reliance upon habits of mind whose sanction is that they were formed by 'experience' in the past." (1963)

The *words* of the master were absorbed and repeated in classroom and on platform, in textbooks and articles. The *practice*, however, has generally amounted to a slighting of standards that has been destructive of morale, confusing and frustrating to both instructors and students. It was not John Dewey. It gave a black eye to the concept of progressive education. But the eye of the autocrat, who could see no evil in autocratic governance, glistened as he said, "I told you so. No discipline, no standards." In fact, however, the school was not truly permissive. Rather there was an unblended, confusing mixture of autocracy with lack of standards.

When in 1945 Dr. Spock first published *The Common Sense Book of Baby and Child Care*, he urged parents to "enjoy your baby." He advised them that the child does not have to be sternly trained, that the baby is not frail, nor as helpless as he or she may appear, and that for the happiest results for the baby and the parents "enjoy him as he is—that is how he'll grow up best." The assumption that an infant is a human being from the moment of birth is basic to Spock's approach.

In a country with as many class, regional, ethnic, and religious differences as the United States, this concept may not in practice be so obviously persuasive to some people as it is in theory. The way children are raised is influenced by the way the parents were raised. It is hard sometimes to admit that what was learned with suffering could have been learned in another way, so, it is often believed, one's children too had best learn through suffering. (This may also be a displacement of hostility by parents and teachers to children.) But in the matrix of a culture that was unconsciously as much as consciously digesting Freud and Dewey and that in its escape from Victorianism was susceptible to all stimuli toward "permissiveness," Spock was regarded as a welcome authority for laissez-faire child rearing.

Watson points out that Spock in his "excellent advice and suggestions on how to avoid 'show-downs with willful children,' " maintains that the child must " 'learn who is boss' while achieving useful channels for aggression. Although direction must be given, there is no need to drive a child into frightening temper tantrums or cow him for all time. There are less painful ways to learn the reality of social surroundings." (Watson 1968) This was often forgotten. So Spock had to emphasize in the 1957 edition of his book "the need that the child has for firm leadership from parents, because this not only makes a better behaved child but a happier child." (Spock 1968) Because a child (or adult) does not require commands, it does not mean that a child (or an adult) does not require guidelines, standards, and models to feel secure and to be "not only better behaved" but also happier.

In practice there has been a considerable ambivalence with regard to teaching the lesson "who is boss." This itself is a confusing, in fact dangerous, concept without Watson's modifying thought "while achieving useful channels for aggression," the opportunity for counterattack. Occasion and temperament (and sometimes child behavior) often determine crackdown by the parents. This is all the more damaging to the developing personalities of children because the occasions for crackdown and permissiveness are generally not ritualized, are unpredictable. In the later edition of his book, Spock felt it necessary to put greater emphasis on the importance of parents teaching their children that parents too had rights.

To live with some satisfaction in society people have to be given norms and values, or they will flounder. They will feel a lack of identity. And when children grow through adolescence to young adulthood and must face people and situations that are not permissive they will be hostile, for they will feel frustrated when they find that behavior and ideas formerly acceptable as incidental to immaturity will no longer be so regarded. They will counterattack when their weak egos cannot cope with the conflict between impulse and the demand of society for order. Erikson says this when he counterposes integrity vs. despair, identity vs. role confusion, and intimacy vs. isolation. (Erikson 1963) Freud in Civilization and Its Discontents (1962) comments on the "sin" of not preparing young people "for the aggressiveness of which they are destined to become the objects." He says that young people are sent into life with an education that is "as though one were to equip people starting on a Polar expedition, with summer clothing and maps of the Italian Lakes." Freud knew more about middle-class children than about the children of the poor whose subculture is more involved with physical aggression than the middle class. Children of the slums are often well cognizant of aggression of various kinds from early childhood.

In a discussion of intelligence Holt expresses this concept in a better way:

> By intelligence we mean a style of life, a way of behaving in various situations, and particularly in new, strange, and perplexing situations. The true test of intelligence is not how much we know how to do, but how we behave when we don't know what to do. (Holt 1982)

Such intelligence, such "style of life," would not be possible unless anchored on values and guided by standards.

Hostility in a Laissez-Faire Situation

A laissez-faire climate in the Lewin, Lippitt, and White experiment (a form of permissiveness) developed a high degree of hostility, not quite as high as the autocratic climate but considerably higher than the democratic. Laissez-faire was less organized, less efficient, and less satisfying to the boys than was the democratic. Less and poorer work was done. There was more absorption in their work by what they called the democratic groups. Involvement by the democratic groups was 50 percent of the total time and only 33 percent of the laissez-faire group. Out and out loafing in the democratic group was 0.2 percent, and in the laissez-faire, 5 percent of the time.

Among the boys who reacted aggressively in the autocratic groups, discontent was expressed 4.4 times per meeting, 3.1 in laissez-faire groups, and only 0.8 in the democratic. "The lack of active guiding suggestions in laissez-faire often resulted in disorganization and in failure and setbacks in work, which were discouraging and exasperating. Some outright aggression can be directly attributed to such work failures, as well as much loss of interest in the job that was being done." (Cartwright and Zander 1960)

When there are neither internal nor external controls, individuals lose a sense of equilibrium, and where there is little or no identity with peers or sense of group solidarity, group norms appear irrelevant. Freedom from outside controls is a comforting dream, but realistically people find little comfort in large doses of permissiveness. They need the support of some structure. Disoriented, they lack a sense of social power. They feel threatened.

In a study of "threat-oriented reactions to power," the subjects who felt ambiguity were less secure, indicated more anxiety, tended to perceive more negatively the power figure, and felt that the impression they had made on him was much worse than that felt by those in a structured condition. They were also less motivated to do well toward the end of the session and had more generalized aggression. "We may say, then," Cohen summarized, "that the exercise of power in an ambiguous situation can provide a great deal of threat for the person who is attempting to reach some sort of need satisfaction." (Cohen 1966) Ambiguity, an absence of standards, can result in feelings of threat, and a need for flight or fight, evasion or hostility.

If they are not threatened, are children bored by permissiveness? Do they find in escapades and crime, in various forms of delinquent behavior, a sense of power they cannot feel where standards of accomplishment are lax? Watt (1975) refers to an experiment with animals who learned to control their environment by pressing levers by which they were able to select conditions other than optimal. When "confronted with a choice of living constantly in an optimal world but being bored or of living in a world that is only optimal part of the time and experiencing variety, even a small rodent will opt for variety." "Perhaps," Watt concludes, "diversity is not merely a luxury for us. It may be something we need." It takes little experience with children to know their need for variety and choices that can offer opportunities for variety. Neither highly structured nor unstructured situations can satisfy this need.

This same need for some form of structure as well as variety is true for administrators. A completely unstructured situation can be painful to most people.

... People (and rats) find the most interest in situations that are neither completely strange nor entirely known—

> where there is novelty to be explored, but where similarities and programs remembered from past experience help guide the exploration. Nor does creativity flourish in completely unstructured situations. (Simon 1960)

A residue of laissez-faire philosophy still permeates much of our social thought. In the climate of business affairs Adam Smith's theory of laissez-faire has not died. This is part of our American free enterprise mind and is ludicrous today when applied to industry and business. Their demand for independence, for free enterprise, prevails only so long as they are not threatened by foreign or domestic competition or risk bankruptcy due to mismanagement or a failure to keep technologies up-to-date. Nevertheless, the myth of laissez-faire still permeates the feelings of young and old about interference by authority in the conduct of business and life. It is a conflict-producing element in the American ethos.

Is it that we dream of an Eden of permissiveness in an attempt to escape from autocracy without assuming the responsibilities and powers of democracy? If so, the dream must fail to be realized. It must result in disillusionment and anger.

We may conclude that neither in our schools nor in other social institutions is there really permissiveness. Even though our inquisitive and creative forces demand variety, these cannot develop in ambiguity.

3 What Children Bring

Imagination and Curiosity

Recently a friend of mine, having outgrown play school, entered kindergarten in the school in which her sister was in the third grade. My friend was beaming, for here was a grander league. She was big enough to be in a regular school. She had achieved. She looked forward to a new experience and many years in which she would learn *something*: to read, to do things with numbers, to play, and do what big children did. Here was hope, a common hope, untouched by frustration, disappointment, or antagonism. When she got to the third grade, she disliked school because "The teacher yells at us."

Another friend was met at the door of her kindergarten class the first day by the teacher, who said to her, "I'm so glad to see you, Linda. I'm so glad you're going to be in my class." Here was welcome; here too was hope, something new, and, of course, it lessened the anxiety that accompanies a new experience.

It is often different. I have been in school offices the opening day of school, waiting to see the principal. There were parents waiting too, to enter their children. We were told by a stern—probably harassed—clerk who did not ask names: "Sit down and wait your turn." The pepper of increased anxiety was spread on the hopes of parents and of children, the first touch of bureaucracy demeaning the new feeling of bigness.

A hearty welcome opens the world. A glum or rejecting reception seeds hostility. It lays a foundation for a defensive wall and counterrejection. This may sound simplistic and indeed it is; nevertheless it is at the heart of our educational dilemma, and it is not often in the consciousness of a bureaucrat who also may have anxieties.

We think of the body of the young child as vulnerable, but consider much less the vulnerability of the young child's mind and feelings. His or her dream life may be invisible to us; certainly it is not what is generally accepted as reality; but reality and dreams may be interchangeable. What might well be schizophrenic in an older person may be the nub of thought, the beginning of creativity, the start of inspired imagination in the very young.

The past means little to a child who has not yet had much of it personally. It is more important to older people who must adjust to it as much as to the present, who must adapt what is happening to what has happened (their experience) and find adjustments to the dissonances between the choices they have made among their values.

So the young place a screen between themselves and history, which they may tend to ignore but cannot escape; while to older people the future appears faded; its pieces do not seem to fit in the jigsaw puzzle they expected to make into a coherent picture.

A difference in approach to the here and now, as well as experience and a sense of history, affects the interaction of children and adults. Children may know more about living in the present world than the ablest adults who, after all, were brought up in a different world. To children airplane travel, television, and computers are not novelties, not innovations to which they have to adapt, but are part of the cultural environment of their lives. In a sense children are aborigines in today, and we, their parents and teachers, immigrants.

To such disparities, as parents and teachers, we may bring little imagination about the inner life of the child, and we may have little patience with what is important to him or her. A poem by Chang-Wou-Kein (1929) describes this fantasy life of a young child and a mother's reaction:

> He sings to put himself to sleep.
> Bending over him, his mother scolds.
>   But he wants, first, to put his song to sleep.

In *Hard Times*, Dickens (1965) describes how school can destroy imagination:

> When she was half-a-dozen years younger, Louisa had been overheard to begin a conversation with her brother one day by saying, "Tom, I wonder"—upon which Mr. Gradgrind, who was the person overhearing, stepped forth into the light and said, "Louisa, never wonder!"
>
> Herein lay the spring of the mechanical art and mystery of educating the reason without stooping to cultivation of the sentiments and affections. Never wonder. By means of addition, subtraction, multiplication, and division, settle everything somehow, and never wonder. Bring to me, says McChoakumchild, yonder baby just able to walk, and I will engage that it shall never wonder. . . .

While, in Mr. Gradgrind, Dickens draws a cartoon, a parody of an unimaginative educator, one can recognize in this a sketch of many a teacher who consciously or unconsciously feels annoyed or threatened if children think beyond the boundaries he or she has set for them in the lesson. After a bell rings that is another matter though; it can be safely assumed that the bell's break in the time-span will almost always break a line of thought. Equally frequently, it will be a relief.

In the course of a sixth-grade class in arithmetic, the teacher asked what "infinity" was. Billy replied, "I think it is like a box of Cream of Wheat." The teacher: "Billy don't be silly!" This left Billy with a sense of aloneness and helplessness and a feeling that his imagination was a threat. Later he said to a psychiatrist, in explanation of why he thought infinity was like a box of Cream of Wheat, "Well . . . think of a box of Cream of Wheat. It shows a man holding a box of Cream of Wheat. Right? And that box shows the same man holding the same box. Right?

And that box . . . You can't see them all, but you can't see infinity. You just know they're all there, going on forever and ever." (Jones 1968)

It is often difficult for a teacher, or any adult, to distinguish between silliness and imagination. But if the first reaction is to dismiss any unexpected response as silly, this is a lesson in outlawing imagination and with it creativity. (Note once more Einstein's comment on how the German schools destroyed creativity.) The story of Billy is an example of failure to meet a child on his own ground, to communicate with him in his own idiom. And one may well wonder whether there is not a place for silliness. Can it not be regarded by a teacher as a verbal or behavioral release from frustration? For silliness can be another form of counterattack to reestablish the child's sense of power, whereas to call him silly may be a lesson leading to alienation.

Jones has pointed out that a crucial element in instruction may be comparison between "significant and believable points" in "the unfamiliar worlds, as brought to the child by the instructional materials, and the familiar worlds, as brought *by* the child *to* the instructional materials." He refers to Piaget's "truism" that "children adapt to knowledge by accommodating it *and* by assimilating it."

An example of how the weight of bureaucracy may pound on independent thought is the case of Martin Woodhams, a thirteen-year-old boy in a British school. He wrote an essay on his family life and his expectations to be a bank clerk, play football, fish, find a girlfriend, make money, go to the continent, live in the jungle like Tarzan, bring back animals, kill lions, buy a cruiser, and live in England with his trophies. "But also this is a dream, a dream world, just a dream world. So as I have had my dreams, I shall go back to work as a public lavatory cleaner."

He and several other children who had turned in essays were picked out by the headmaster for criticism as "obscene, flippant and derisory." He ordered them, five girls included, to come in and be caned. Martin refused. He said he thought the words "public lavatory cleaner" seemed rude to the headmaster but were not so to him.

So Martin was suspended. He stayed home for a month. The school's board of governors considered his case and a majority voted to uphold the headmaster and insist that Martin accept punishment or move to another school. He stayed home.

Of course Martin's reference to work as a public lavatory cleaner was not rude or flippant. It was a poignant expression of the dreams and hopelessness of a working-class English boy. It was his imagination more than his body that was to be flogged and he courageously defied the authorities for the sake of his imagination. (Lewis 1971)

When an adult is not aware that such dream lives exist and fails to understand the general differences in symbolic comprehension, a child must feel misjudged and rejected. It is disturbing that although the whole business of teaching is in terms of symbols—words, pictures, numbers, formulas, musical notation—teachers have so little awareness of the symbolic meaning to the students of the substance of learning or, if aware, so little capacity or available energy to pursue the comparative meanings of the symbols to themselves and their students. What opportunities there are in such comparisons to illustrate how misunderstandings occur and how awareness can lead to conflict resolution.

We all have dream lives that we must reconcile with or test against reality or, failing, become involved in a schizophrenic state. In young children the line between dream and reality is not yet sharp, and understanding is needed to educate, to draw out an appreciation of the differences.

Children are not rejected only by adults; or, rather, behavior that a child may interpret as rejection is not only that of adults. Other children may create the same feeling, picking on some deviance, something unacceptable, as a cue to hostile response. We see this in the haiku by Shiki (1960):

> *That snotty urchin*
> *Left unpicked by either team.*
> *Ah the bitter cold!*

They can treat each other with torturing cruelty. Children may reject other children because they are "too smart" or imaginative. To avoid this many youngsters try to hide their intelligence, what they read at home, and what they really think. Life among their peers may be better if they are graded B rather than the A of which they are capable.

Some Adult Expectations

Most of us assume, or at least hope, that once it is pointed out, children will accept the significance of what is taught as being the same significance we see. If children learn a fact it is assumed that it will be assimilated and that if they are of normal intelligence and not "contrary," they will accommodate themselves and their thinking to the fact. The teacher might not, of course, expect the same of adults. For as Augustine pointed out, teachers may present models to children that they do not expect adults to follow. (Augustine 1943)

Whatever their origins teachers have incorporated into their thinking and expectations American middle-class values such as: (1) economic success as a measure of social acceptance and happiness; (2) a consumer economy in which to outbid others for currently acceptable goods and ideas; (3) respect of property; and (4) achievement without violence (except in defense of differing values).

However, the values and expectations of the teacher may not be at all acceptable to the children, especially to the slum children, black, white, Asian, or Latino, and to American Indians. What a teacher assumes should motivate children may not in fact motivate them. Their home culture may be apathetic or hostile. As the teacher is the authority it will be the child who is deemed wrong and insubordinate, perhaps labeled delinquent. The typical teaching situation is a win-lose one, with the teacher holding the power to win. For the teacher holds not only the rewards and punishment of marks, promotion, and suspension but also great psychological rewards and punishments in terms of how the student is received or rejected.

It would appear to be a poor learning situation when students feel they must try to satisfy the teacher rather than themselves. *What children want to know is answers to their own questions.* These may be questions originating directly from their own curiosity or indirectly stimulated by the teacher—not the uninspiring questions teachers base on the text that are checkups on the students or substitutes for teachers' imaginations.

The parents of a young friend of mine received a report on her achievements in nursery school. It complimented her on having followed *instructions* in coloring pictures. I was distressed by this, not knowing how the teacher interpreted "instructions." I remembered a boy who was excellent in art but who had been instructed in art class to draw a glass half full of water, which he could do before the assignment. It bored him. I suggested that perhaps he could draw a flower in the glass of water, but he assured me that the teacher would not accept any variation from the assignment. To "instruct" has several meanings: one, to teach, and the other, to direct. If the instruction were to teach it would be to help the child to do effectively what he or she was motivated to do, that is, to assist him or her to learn the techniques necessary to answer his or her questions or create what he or she wanted to create. But if the instruction is a direction to the child to do what the teacher wants him or her to do, eventually it will destroy imagination and initiative and stimulate conflict, whether expressed or repressed. Instruction can be a helping art; it ought not be regimentation. The latter induces hostility. Admittedly the line between instruction that is helping and instruction that regiments is a thin one. To achieve the benefit of some stability by the achievement of a set, uniform standard, the price may be rigidity and the rejection of imagination.

We must face the reality, however, that adults for the most part, and teachers especially, traditionally have a skewed expectation that education requires docility in children. This is illustrated by definitions of the word *docile:* teachable, submissive, easily managed, amenable to training, tractable.* Yes, indeed, follow instructions! But is such docility a formula for a democracy; or rather is it a prescription for generating a capacity to adapt to authority without hostile behavior in order to achieve an outwardly less hostile balance of power?

Students are expected to devour without digesting and eliminate without absorbing prefabricated information, to be docile. And one who does his or her own thinking and evaluating learns to accept and adapt, replicating the teacher's truisms for survival but withholding what is his or hers in some secret closet of mind and feeling until it is safe to release it. Perhaps more often a student will submit, surrender independent judgment, smother dissent and sense of power. Consciously or unconsciously a sense of guilt will grow with a need to counterattack in some manner, somewhere. The kitchen chair may release hostility even though it be only the symbol of a kicked shin. Counterattack may be overt; or it may be by way of contempt for teacher, self, and learning. By contempt of another it is possible to resolve cognitive dissonance, to reestablish a sense of power.

Adaptation

I am told this story by a mother who conferred with her daughter's English teacher. It is an example of a common method of student adaptation. The report of the daughter's work and behavior was good. The teacher's only criticism was that the girl did not volunteer any answers in the literature "discussion." When the mother repeated this to her daughter she said that her interpretations did not coincide with her teacher's and that the teacher would only accept the "correct" answer. Therefore, she would continue to refuse orally to feed the teacher answers that were unacceptable to her (the daughter) but, in order to get the best possible mark, would give the

---

*See *The Concise Oxford Dictionary* (Oxford: At the Clarendon Press, 1938); *Funk & Wagnalls Standard College Dictionary* (New York: Funk & Wagnalls, 1966).

desired answers on the written examinations. This incident occurred in a seventh-eighth grade accelerated class, that is, a class for bright children. Children learn quickly the social skill of impressing teachers (and parents) to get their approval.

Motivation to Learn

An important stimulus to learning is the desire to please the teacher and the parents to whom the teacher may stand, to some extent, as surrogate. This desire to please somebody with authority is learned long before the child enters school and the pattern continues long after he or she has left school. Additional motives for learning may be the expectation of obtaining answers to the child's curiosity concerning physical phenomena he or she does not understand (especially in the generally outlawed subject of sex). There is also the wish to gain increased power and authority which appear to be within the control of superiors. And there is the stimulation to use expanding powers to handle new situations. (Menninger 1942)

> The underlying need to be dependent usually is in sharp conflict with the desire to be mature, causing an inner sense of insecurity and a reaction of impotent rage. The individual may try to overcompensate through a lust for power. . . . (Saul 1949)

Adolescents feel their oats without yet learning the capacity to postpone gratification or the ecological aspects of all behavior, that is, its effect on others, or an appreciation of the situation in which the behavior occurs.

Many children want to learn to read for the sake of reading, and to solve mathematical problems for the sake of finding solutions. Many others find satisfaction in less intellectual experiences. They may learn to read or figure more readily if it helps them to mastery and better understanding of the arts or to learn mathematics to work with computers or other forms of technology. This would suggest the value of studies not considered "basics"—art, music, mechanics, for example—as avenues to "basic" learning. Teachers and students are so various and so gloriously different that it is axiomatic that they must read differently in response to their personalities as well as to their ages, experiences, and, therefore, their perceptions. To expect identical achievement of success must surely be irrelevant. Success has many stages, situations, and, of course, definitions.

Generally the child goes through school, from elementary school on, with the hope of growing more competent, having more choices in life, the possibility of earning money, gaining status, and political and other forms of power. The expectation of realizing such hopes tends, however, to diminish.

There will be disillusionment, a strong sense of comparative deprivation and hostility if jobs are scarce, pay low, and the chance of political participation minimal. Then one will often find acceptance limited to acceptance by parasitic or hostile people. The road from failure to disillusionment at the end of a tattered rainbow is a journey to hostility. Moreover, when one is young, poor, and especially if one is a member of some rejected (or unaccepted) minority group, this end result of failure may become all the more apparent. If children live in a culture of violence, as is so often the case in the black ghettos and the barrios, violence may become an acceptable resource. And they continually see examples of violent acts and corruption that have been done with impunity without ever being apprehended or punished. "It takes rather little energy . . . to enable a human being to destroy others or the integration of a society." (Bateson 1979)

Schools cannot be expected and should not try to solve all social or personal problems. But we may ask of them the question, have you strengthened or destroyed the self-respect and social responsibility of your pupils?

Another aspect is fear and the anticipation of punishment learned very early. As David Bowers said, "Fear . . . is never associated with learning what to do, but rather what not to do," that is, what to avoid. (Bowers 1977)* He suggests this sequence

---

*Bowers is talking about employee-employer relationships, but the same pattern is relevant to any superior-subordinate relationship.

of events: (a) Directive A from a superior will tell the subordinate what to do; (b) the reaction is, however, "When I hear Directive A I must avoid being held responsible for the nonexistence of Directive A's outcome." (As will be discussed later this formula is as relevant to teacher-supervisor relationships as it is to teacher-student relationships.)

The example of the girl in the grade-school English class illustrates this. She wishes to gain her teacher's approval (love) by expressing her own ideas, her own values. However, she is afraid to do this. She must avoid retribution if she does so, because her teacher does not accept disagreement. This is a lesson in avoidance of responsibility, of a culture of the "Don't blame me" syndrome that affects society at large (see chapter 5).

Sex Difference and Learning

From infancy boys and girls tend to have different capacities and reactions. The pattern of schooling affects boys and girls differently. As now conceived it is more frustrating for boys. The competency of girls is generally displayed through the fine motor system which leads them to superiority at an early age in speech and "visual images for two-dimensional space." Boys' competency tends to display itself through the gross motor system. They have a better sense of three-dimensional objects and they like to take things apart. In a study of children three to four and a half years old who were observed for twenty minutes each, several girls but only one boy were consistently engaged in one activity for the period.

> The average time that girls worked at the same project was 12.5 minutes; for the boys it was 6.5 minutes. During the entire period, girls played at an average of two and a half activities; boys, at five and a half. Boys interrupted what they were doing twice as often as the girls. Although girls finished most of the projects they began, boys finished only half. (McGuinness 1979)

The perceptual, motor, and social differences between the sexes affect the development of intellectual abilities. When children "are expected to behave like girls" they are required to be attentive to one task, to remain seated in one place, and to receive auditory information at the beginning of each task. Writing and drawing utilize the fine motor systems and are largely linguistic and symbolic. The attention span of boys being shorter, they find it more difficult to adapt to school requirements. Furthermore, males tend to be more interested in objects and nonsocial events and females are more sensitive to social cues and people. Our civilization tends to reinforce these traits.

More than 90 percent of hyperactive children are males. The requirements of the classroom are therefore much more repressive of boys for they have little chance during class to express gross motor movements. In other words, our classrooms generally "are geared to skills that come naturally to girls but develop very slowly in boys." (Restak 1979) Boys' potentialities are usually not given sufficient opportunities, with the result of a feeling of reduced sense of power. Therefore, it is not surprising that the hostility aroused in boys will be expressed so frequently in physical activity and often in violent actions. May not the misbehavior of boys often be a result of the requirement that they suppress their need for more physical activity and the failures of most teaching to encourage them to learn by "taking things apart," whether objects or ideas? But, in any event, until school practices are modified, boys will continue to be more antagonistic to school.

These differences in male and female capacities do not uniformly apply to either sex. Nor do they in any way imply that one sex is superior to another, but rather that they begin with innate differences and may require different handling in classrooms. Boys can be helped to achieve verbal skills, girls mathematical and mechanical skills. After all, men *are* writers and increasingly women enter professions requiring high competence in mathematics.

Junior High School as a Flash Point

It is generally accepted that young people of junior-high-school age—say eleven to fourteen—are the most difficult with whom schools have to deal. This period becomes a flash point of hostility. There are great variations in the development of these children. An eleven-year-old may be two years younger or two or three years older in development than the norm. Bodily changes precipitate feelings of adulthood which are contradicted by continuing need for dependence. The age of puberty has tended to go downward within the last few decades. This age group is especially sensitive to being treated as children. Interest in the opposite sex and a feeling of their own sex develop. They have unanswered but vital questions about sex which adults so often hesitate to discuss frankly with them and object to schools teaching, claiming, not improperly, that sex is a subject for parental instruction, though parents may default.

Youngsters in early adolescence begin developing the capacity for critical thinking and for making ethical decisions, that is, they consciously adopt their own value systems. They have a need to test or prove themselves and develop new skills; and, expressed or unexpressed, they demand a share in decision making about their lives and education. The curriculum and atmosphere of the junior high school inhibit them. The curriculum is rarely flexible, rarely adaptable to their genesis of adulthood. It lacks the excitement they are seeking in all facets of their lives.

Although adolescents may feel more competent than they are, they are, in fact, more competent than they were. Our frequent failure to recognize their growing capabilities leaves them with a sense of futility and the feeling that they have been deprived of power over their own lives. They counterattack. It is not surprising that this group has the highest rate of school crime such as vandalism.

> . . . The traditional junior high school tends to value its students less for what they are than for what they can produce—in academic or athletic achievement. Most youth-serving agencies have considered it their mission to do things *to* or *for* their clients, rather than encouraging them to develop their ability to help themselves. (*New Roles for Early Adolescents* 1981)

Under adult guidance that is sympathetic and enthusiastic, the problems of these young people can be met with programs that are not child's play but have a real outcome for them. Some such programs have been effectively developed and put into practice by the National Commission on Resources for Youth in junior high schools in urban and in rural districts in many parts of the country. They involve such activities as:

Working as tutors in elementary schools

Being museum guides and assisting museum curators

Working on farms and leading tours of handicapped children on farms

Young adolescents with learning disabilities and behavioral problems tutoring other youngsters with similar difficulties

Assisting bilingual classes in the elementary schools, by teaching their native languages to English speaking children

Acting as reporters broadcasting TV news programs

Building a geodesic dome

With the aid of the National Council of Christians and Jews, helping to improve the relationships between blacks and whites in North Carolina

In Portland, Oregon, after being trained by school and police officers, presenting to other classes information on such matters as property safety, drugs, school problems, vandalism, shop lifting, etc. (In the pilot school of this program broken window damage each summer amounted to $300 to $400. During the summer of 1980, when the program was in effect, there was none.)

After a semester of studying with professionals on the site of a garden, conducting tours of visiting elementary school groups

In every one of these projects early adolescents have seen a real outcome and they have had the satisfaction of helping others. They have been under adult guidance and they have participated in planning their project. Do the youngsters who have participated in these programs learn traditional lessons better? This requires more research. One would assume they did; book learning could be related to their broader social experience. Certainly such programs should reduce hostility by recognition of the capacities of the young people and by acceptance of them as being no longer babies.

Unfortunately, there has been no formal evaluation of these programs but the adult leaders and the young participants have agreed, among other things, that vandalism has been reduced where these programs have existed. In the program in the Minneapolis public schools, experience in health-care occupations has been integrated with the health-science learning program for minority and disadvantaged students; and the average class attendance for those students was 81 percent as compared with 66 percent to 71 percent in the city's other alternative programs.

Programs such as these are of a different quality from what is sometimes called "work experience." According to Professor John J. Mitchell:

> . . . The difference between these two terms is important because during the past decade "work experience" has become a label for a wide assortment of youth projects which are tedious at the personal level and insignificant at the societal level. Work experience of this sort serves no developmental function for adolescents and, in the long run, probably encourages worker alienation more than it reduces it. Work merely for the sake of work is not what Youth Participation is about. Youth involvement projects which are trivial, boring, or non-significant in their societal contribution are not worth the adult energy required to run them! (*New Roles for Early Adolescents* 1981)

Youth-oriented projects, such as those mentioned, have resulted in findings that "youngsters consistently prove to be
more innovative, intelligent, and industrious than is predicted
by the 'experts.' " (*New Roles for Early Adolescents* 1981) Outside agencies can be of help to schools; but it is better if schools
enable teachers and principals to have sufficient independence, sufficient professional life-space, to be creative.

The program just described is a sample of many valuable
experimental programs in our schools—probably thousands of
them. Unfortunately, really adequate evaluations of their successes and failures are generally lacking and successes have not
been adequately publicized so that they have remained local
experiences.

There are many teachers who are imaginative and who would
be creative in many ways we cannot guess if they had support;
and if they were not to be intimidated by demands for submissive conformity as, for instance, by pressures to have their
classes do well on standardized tests. Such tests may be a sort
of balance sheet, but like any balance sheet do not often reveal
thinking capacity, imagination, or the capacity to work well
with others.

Failure

In a report by the Vera Institute of Justice (Strasburg 1978),
it was found that there were schools in which bored, underedu-
cated children incapable of reading and writing were advanced
grade by grade through the system to the tenth or eleventh
grade, when they were subjected to pressure to leave school so
that the school did not have to award them diplomas. This, the
study said, was at a minimum a failure to act responsibly and
professionally in the identification of pupils' problems though,
of course, many could not be dealt with and should not be
attempted to be dealt with in regular classes. "Students han-
dled in this manner realize that they are being ignored and
misled, which can only increase their frustration and disdain
for the society around them."

Daniel Glaser (1975) "found considerable evidence of strong associations between conflict with school authorities, poor performance in aptitude tests, poor grades, and student dislike of school on the one hand and delinquency on the other." The hostility, the need to counterattack (see chapter 1) may be brought to the school, but the finding that delinquency becomes less when these young people leave school is suggestive.

The student most likely to succeed is the one who can solve problems as problems, whether or not they are abstract and divorced from personal or other human problems. Large numbers of students are unable to achieve competence in such skills and proceed through school, others leave with a sense of failure. To such children school becomes especially hateful because they are forced to do things in which they fail over and over. The older they are the more they become aware that they are failing, that they are being considered stupid and not worthy of attention. (Donaldson 1979)

To defend themselves against feeling to be failures, many students—and adults too—do not try. In this way failure can be attributed to lack of effort, a bravado of "I-didn't-even-try," rather than to lack of ability. Not trying can provide relief from anxieties of failure or a sense of being stupid, though usually only temporarily; for if not trying, or a belief it is not worth trying, becomes a pattern of life, it cuts off the possibility of success. Except for the intervention of the uncertain element of luck, there can be little success without trying and little satisfaction without some effort to overcome. The self-indulgent or spoiled child tends to avoid effort and misses satisfaction, even if he or she is bright. Not trying can in itself be a hostile act resulting from a self-imposed sense of loss of social power and self-created sense of comparative deprivation.

Most children, even many failures, come to like something about school. It may be a teacher or more often some companion, some peer. It may be a subject studied with a sense of achievement, or sports, or drama, or some other extracurricular activity through which they can find self-expression. Even for such children there is likely to be a sense at some time or other of entrapment in a system established by authorities they cannot control and conducted by authorities most of whom are invisible and those visible frequently punitive.

Frustration of Silence

According to Goodlad "the average instructional day in a junior or senior high school includes 150 minutes of talking. Of this, only seven minutes is initiated by students." (Goodlad 1983)

We ask children to answer questions not to ask them—except in the context of what they have been "taught." We offer them what we believe they should learn without also stimulating them to imagine and inquire, both innate needs. Some have the capacity to avoid the drain of imagination and inquiry; they lead double lives, that of the school and their own. Others rebel and are lost—although occasionally some rebels may become leaders in government or gangs; and most succumb to pro forma schooling and the culture of soap operas and dramas of violence. There can be little sense of social power in listening continually to others with rare opportunities to express one's self and get one's questions heard and respected. We forget, don't we, that the "why?" so essential to the small child's learning is equally important to more mature persons.

The brightest, most successful students, as well as the unsuccessful, frequently find the last year of high school a bore, a frustration of their state of genesis. It appears to them to be an impediment to achieving a greater sense of maturity through holding a job (earning money) or entering college. Often it occurs to them: what's the use of it all? What value is school to those who see no employment opportunities or further education? How can schools help these young people find the final year of high school emotionally as well as intellectually rewarding? How much are they consulted? Would it not help to motivate them if their questions were encouraged, and answered, and their opinions sought? They would be less frustrated if they could talk more of the time. (How much that schools might do are the schools denied the opportunity to do because the great economic and social problems are deemed "political" by vocal members of their communities? It has been claimed that nuclear armaments and their dangers are matters too "political" to be considered by children.)

Could not school be made more attractive to high-school students, more relevant to their lives and hopes, if they were consulted in the construction of the curriculum and if the learning they get outside of school were integrated with what teachers attempt to offer within the classroom? Perhaps programs such as those of the National Commission on Resources for Youth, already discussed, may be appropriate for some high-school as well as junior-high-school students. By high-school age earning money has become a symbol of achievement, so that what may satisfy young adolescents in nonremunerative service may have less appeal to older adolescents. Children from well-to-do families, as well as those less affluent, seek summer jobs that pay.

Children are dreamers, wonderers, experimenters, inquirers, adapters, rebels, or submitters, desiring achievement, some power, love, and avoidance of blame. Consequently, their more imperative needs and interests may not mesh well with the offerings of school. Frustration and counterattack, therefore, would seem to be unavoidable. How much is helpful, how much destructive? How and in what circumstances does hostility take precedence? How can this be minimized? These questions require empirical research. We are not close to answers.

4 Weight of Poverty

Poverty and Slum Life

Above all poverty itself and its many deprivations emphasize the relativity of opportunity. Lack of nourishment, lack of decent clothing, and lack of a chance of privacy illustrate this. (Like the child we knew who could only find "privacy" to do her homework in her family's small apartment by sitting on top of the refrigerator.)

I recall the case of a high-school girl who refused to change to gymnasium clothes for a physical education class. She was scolded by the teacher, and on her continued refusal to do as the others did, was sent to the principal for punishment. He was a sympathetic person and finally she was able to tell him that she could not afford a gym suit, and, even so, she was ashamed to let the other girls see the condition of her underwear. Clothing may be a highly competitive area. (The current habit of simple—not designer—blue jeans is a healthy equalizer however unattractive they may often appear.)

Children of the slums do not share the prevailing middle-class American culture. To them violence is often an everyday interaction, among them literacy is at a lower level, and middle-class experience is secondary through television and the movies. They grow up in one or another slum culture. Of that Dubos wrote:

> [It] is not accurate to state that slum children are cultur-
> ally deprived; the more painful truth is that slum life im-
> prints on them a culture from which they are usually
> unable to escape. (Dubos 1968)

There are parents who themselves may have suffered from the stresses of childhoods in slums. The physical and emotional damages that have been theirs may find them less able to offer the nurturing care needed to protect their children from further damage. (Strasburg 1978) Their children inherit poverty and its cultures as others inherit a bank account and library.

The style and condition of clothing may present an emotional deprivation causing discomfort, jealousy, or anger. Inadequate nutrition, however, causes physical and cognitive deprivation as well as emotional.

Nutrition, Learning, and Behavior

Malnutrition and undernutrition are critical contributors to the culture of poverty, and, therefore, the ills of malnutrition tend to grip generation after generation of the poor and limit their access to rights of life and liberty, to jobs, and to a good education.

Older children as well as infants who are malnourished or inadequately nourished tend to exhibit more behavioral problems than adequately nourished children. They tend toward apathy, lethargy, listlessness, inability to pay attention, and fearfulness in social situations, which makes it difficult for them to learn in school and to hold jobs. (Winick 1969)

Experience has shown that free breakfast programs as well as free lunch programs have improved the span of attention and learning capacity of children. There is a mass of evidence to the effect that malnutrition is an important source of learning disability and behavioral problems in the schoolroom. (Meyers et al. 1968)

Nutrition is definitely related to intellectual performance:

> This may be the greatest impact that nutrition has on intellectual performance—not an effect on "innate ability" or "general intelligence" but on the utilization of the ability that the child does have and if the child does not learn early what the school expects him to learn he will be forever handicapped in educational progression. (Kallen 1971)

It is indisputable that hunger makes children dull even though there may be no evidence that feeding people adequately makes them "smart."

The brain grows by cell division that determines the number of brain cells developed, and also by an increase in the size of the cells. In a child seriously malnourished in utero or during the first year or two after birth, brain growth is retarded because the brain-cell division does not occur normally and there is interference with the development of the normal size of the brain cells. (Dayton 1969; Winick 1970) Scientific evidence strongly supports the conclusion that such malnutrition is a cause of retarded intellectual development. (Chase and Martin 1970) Poverty not genetics, therefore, may be a cause of low scores on intelligence tests; and poverty is not confined to any race or any slum, call it ghetto, barrio, or Appalachia.

Although such brain deficiencies are not genetic they may be culturally inheritable, in that, women who themselves have been malnourished in utero or infancy may bear children with underdeveloped brains, regardless of whether the mothers were adequately nourished later in life, even during their own pregnancies. (*Maternal Nutrition and Family Planning in the Americas* 1970; Gruenwald 1971)

Probably brain deficiency is more likely to lead to apathy, as mentioned above, than to hostility, although there are few who will not under some pressures respond hostilely. In any event, undernourished children tend to have more emotional instability, apathy, listlessness, and inability to pay attention than the adequately nourished. This not only reduces the capacity to learn but may lead to confrontations between frustrated students and frustrated teachers with consequent hostility.

The proper feeding of the population is the concern of federal, state, and local governments. Schools can only act as conduits for those parts of a program that feed children who need breakfasts or luncheons. These programs, together with nutritional assistance to pregnant women and small children, are necessary if the schooling of the poor is to be effective.

If we are to give equal opportunity to education, it may be less of a waste of public funds to feed in school five children whose parents can afford to pay for their meals than to have one hungry child who because of hunger is dull in class or a behavior problem. Quality education of the hungry or those suffering malnutrition cannot reasonab be expected.

There are persons and families that are exceptions, but in the main, life goes on in slums as in a stagnant pool. It is life deviating from what we consider the norm. It is an ecosystem of decay, suffering, discrimination, malnutrition, lack of consumer goods, lack of the delicacies held before all the nation by advertising, and with little opportunity for privacy, and shortage of jobs, especially for young people. Yes, again with exceptions, there are disappointed expectations to realize capacity, sense of loss of social power, and comparative deprivation year after year. It is a life of failure. It is a life of endemic hostility and violence. There are also many people of the slums who give up, lose ambition, and shuffle through life in a sort of dazed indifference.

Children come from this slum life. They go to school, to learn and achieve among people who are often suspicious of them; who frequently discount them; who see their culture at best intellectually or sentimentally; who want to fit them into an already hostile setting; and wonder, often irritably, why reading scores in their schools are below national norms.

> For the larger part of America there is social and economic mobility through the educational system. Beneath that level a line is drawn to an "under-class." That class line becomes demarcated almost as a caste line, since the children in this class tend to become as poorly endowed as their parents. (Myrdal 1963)

Until recently there were employment opportunities in great numbers for people whose capacities were limited to the use of hands and muscles. This is no longer so. "Viewed as a resource in production, a man is a pair of eyes and ears, a brain, a pair of hands, a pair of legs, and some muscles for applying force." (Simon 1964) Now, however, automation performs many functions that were formerly man's and has eliminated some of those. "Thus, man's comparative advantage in energy production has been greatly reduced in most situations—to the point where he is no longer a significant source of power in our economy." His brain, the use of his sensory organs, hands, and the use of his legs in rough terrain still give him a comparative advantage. It is his flexibility in these spheres where he may still have a comparative advantage over the machine. However, even the use of sophisticated machines requires a knowledge of reading and the ability to apply that knowledge. Education for an "under-class" dooms students to this "caste" and inevitably results in a sense of failure and a depreciation of a sense of personal worth.

Many of these children have been relegated to vocational courses, catchalls for those not academically minded. This inevitably results in disappointment and a sense of failure. Vocational training in large measure has been for skills that have become outmoded. A large proportion of vocational trainees do not enter the trades for which they are supposedly trained. In most cases they have to be retrained on the job. Meanwhile, they have been "deprived of some part of the knowledge and understanding, however broadly defined, that constitute the intellectual makeup of educated men and women." (Jackson 1981) If vocational training is not to "be wasted or even block the way to good jobs" (Myrdal 1963), it should be given in conjunction with apprenticeships in industry or commerce. This will require better cooperation among schools, labor unions, and employers. It has been done as, for example, in the cooperative education program in the New York City schools. If some such program does not exist, vocational education will seem to many students a signal that they are regarded as failures and, perhaps, as castaways.

Out of the "Underclass"

Kurtz, dying after living many years among the savages of the Congo, said of life: "The horror!" (Conrad 1977). This might be the summation of slum life. We try to push away recognition of this horror, denying to ourselves its realities. However, we expect schools to handle the children of poverty, of the slum cultures, with the same success, with little deviation of method, as they do other children. We expect teachers to overcome the evils that arise and persist because of our insensitivity, our unreadiness to face what we want them to face, and to make sacrifices we will not make. Children may fail, and when they do it is simpler for us to turn from the horror and place blame and our burden on the schools. Schools cannot be expected to make up for the public's defaults. Neither should they evade their own responsibilities. We can only expect of them that in attempting to give children necessary skills they do not increase hostility by confrontations with the cultural results of the children's homes and neighborhoods. We must expect schools to recognize that children can be handicapped by poverty as by blindness, deafness, or muscular dystrophy.

Today we recognize that schools have a responsibility to modify the regular educational fare of students in order to give special support to those who have seeing, hearing, mental, and mobility disadvantages. We even make provision for those whose native language is not English. We have been attempting, often awkwardly and with many needless confrontations, to reduce the disadvantages of race. An underclass inevitably generates hostility. It automatically inhibits a genesis of youth. *Is it not time that we recognize that the disadvantages, the handicaps, that originate in slums also require especial consideration?*

Whatever special education is given to children it should not be segregated except in rare instances, such as perhaps children of very low intelligence. When in the form of vestibule classes there should be constant intermingling with other children. There should be no sense of isolation, no sense of deprivation because of handicap, no implication of class or race distinction. The trouble with vestibules as well as doorways is that people frequently stay in them and forget that they are two-way passageways.

Other disabilities children bring to school result from broken or truncated homes. An increasingly large proportion of American families consists of a one-parent family. Divorce and desertion are not limited to any economic class. Illegitimate children are mostly from the poorer. Whether the breakup comes from divorce and desertion or a death in the family, or whether from illegitimacy, children suffer and they bring the traumatic effects to school. The children need parenting—emotional support that the remaining parent, especially in the first year or so, may be unable to give. The functional and often financial problems of the remaining parents tend to preoccupy them. Supervision and discipline may become lax. Whether the traumas result from confusion of loyalties, confusion of events, economic disaster, loss of supportiveness, or anything else, children's readjustment to living includes readjustment to the school.

The problems of children from broken homes are important to schools because these children are working "below their academic potential." Most teachers probably understand this but may not have the time, sensitivity, and training to help those children. Full-time counselors for individual students are not usually within budgets of school systems. (Francke 1983) To what extent would group therapy be helpful and available? Talking it out, talking it over with others who can share experiences, would arouse less hostility than the best meant advice. At least temporarily, children from split families may be handicapped. How in this period they are received and supported is likely to make a permanent difference in their lives and learning.

It has been said that to suppose that the "poor are poor because they are poor" is an obfuscation and that the most "desperate and refractory sector of the 'poverty problem,' " is the race problem. (Duncan 1968) Certainly racial discrimination is involved in and may accentuate the problems of poverty. However, poverty is broader than race. There are poor whites in Appalachia and other communities. Their problems in schools, and with an education cut to a middle-class last, also result in denials of a sense of social power.

Martin Luther King, Jr., wrote that "The job of the school is to teach so well that background is no longer an issue." (King 1967) This is all very well but it is difficult to see how schools can teach well if they ignore the backgrounds of the children. Schools, for better or worse, can never be immune to the effects of social, economic, and political environments on children; for those environments are also educational and may support or counter what the schools are trying to teach. When King spoke of the solution of poverty by abolishing it, he was on firmer theoretical ground, however difficult politically and economically this may be. Coleman stated better what perhaps King may have had in mind: "Schools are successful only insofar as they reduce the dependence of a child's opportunities upon his social origins." (Coleman 1966)

Schools, teachers, do not have the divine power to create order out of chaos. Nevertheless, they do have the capacity to look with understanding into the chaos of the slums and stimulate in children a sprouting, a genesis.

5 Youth as a "State of Genesis"

The school's "business should be to teach how to think rather than what to think."

—Price 1980

Importance of Imagination

Daydreams, imagination and creative moments of free consciousness, the unselfconscious poetry or philosophic insight—as in the case of the boy and his Cream of Wheat pictures—are the seedbeds of curiosity. As Carl Sagan said, "Curiosity and the urge to solve problems are the emotional hallmarks of our species. . ." (Sagan 1977) From this point of view the wish to learn is inborn, "a natural process." "[F]rom infancy all normal human beings show signs of a keen desire to learn—a desire that does not appear to depend on any reward apart from the satisfaction of achieving competence and control." (Donaldson 1979) To Menninger a child's motives for learning are a need to exchange love and "expressing in socially approved ways the aggressive tendencies." (Menninger 1942) Whatever the psychological or biological causes, little children do learn to speak, understand, discriminate, sit, and walk without lessons.

What happens to youngsters who enter school with hope, with a sense of achievement, because they are old enough to go to school? Under increasing pressure to conform, their expectations to be treated as more grown-up, more mature, are frequently not realized. Freedom of imagination becomes muffled. A situation of comparative deprivation and loss of social power develops. There is a universal need to feel that one is a worthwhile person, that one's well-being is valued, that one's contribution has importance, and that one is respected, even liked, by those who have importance to him or her. Fulfillment of this need stimulates motivation; nonfulfillment tends to reduce motivation. "Experiences which a person has in the course of his organizational life, and the behavior of others toward him . . . produce a favorable reaction when they enhance that perception, an unfavorable reaction when they reduce or weaken it. . . ." (Bowers 1977) This is especially so when the organization that has authority and power over a person, as the school does over the child, denies a sense of favorable reaction, denies realization that he or she is a worthwhile person.

"Youth likes to be in a state of genesis, of beginning," Buber said. "A young man wants to be able to say, 'I am the first! Not just continuing something my father has done, even if this was glorious in itself.' " (Hodes 1971) That is why curiosity and imagination are so precious to the young and why they have greater importance to them than the past. Perhaps this is one reason why the past which occupies such a large part in education (but also partly because it is poorly presented as the dead past in history lessons) is unreal and unimportant to young people. "[O]ur wishes," Bertrand Russell said, "can affect the future but not the past, the future is to some extent subject to our power, while the past is unalterably fixed. . . . But I think that, in the intoxication of a quick success, much that is required for a true understanding of the universe has been forgotten." (Russell 1957) Youth is so little interested in the past because it is irrelevant to the "sense of genesis."

Referring to letters he had received from young people and their longings and their opposition to authority and dogma, Buber said, "They are dreaming of something they cannot describe and when young people have dreams like these the nameless will take on a shape sooner or later." (Hodes 1971)

Sagan mentions the remarkably gifted multidisciplinary scientists and scholars whom England possessed in this century. And he cites Russell's comment that "the development of such gifted individuals required a childhood period in which there was little or no pressure for conformity, a time in which the child could develop and pursue his or her own interests no matter how unusual or bizarre. . . ." (Sagan 1977) Such freedom is necessary because out of this comes the random. More often that not the random fails. However, "without the random, there can be no new thing." (Bateson 1979)

In another place Sagan (1977) said:

> . . . [T]he future belongs to those societies that, while not ignoring the reptilian and mammalian parts of our being, enable the characteristically human components of our nature to flourish, to those societies that encourage diversity rather than conformity; . . . to those societies that treat new ideas as delicate, fragile and immensely valuable pathways to the future."

Speaking of a bacterium, François Jacob (1973) wrote: "Its perceptions and reactions are reduced to one alternative, yes or no." One may wonder at times if to simplify their tasks some teachers may not regard their students as little different from a bacterium. And, in reverse, the teacher requires little imagination and may hide his or her ignorance if answers to student questions are in effect restricted to yes and no.

The Value of Mistakes

Where there is imagination there will be mistakes. Without imagination there can be no progress, no adaptation, no future. Therefore, the most serious mistake is to submerge imagination.

This is eloquently stated by Lewis Thomas (1979):

> The capacity to blunder slightly is the real marvel of DNA. Without this special attribute, we would still be an-

> human, we say, but we don't like the idea much, and it is harder still to accept the fact that erring is biological as well. . . . But there it is: we are here by the purest chance, and by mistake at that.

We tend to denigrate the importance of error. "The study of error is not only in the highest degree prophylactic but it serves as a stimulating introduction to the study of truth." (Lippmann 1922)

Most mistakes are not as damaging as the blame, the passion for finding a scapegoat, the failure to recognize that in the process of change there must be failure as well as successes. Some people are prone to erring and they may be unfitted to their occupations, for certain activities; but others may be deemed mistaken in the value systems of conservative beholders when, in fact, they are inventive of methods to overcome existing failures. Thousands—perhaps hundreds of thousands—of teachers could improve education if superintendents, colleagues, and the public did not blame them for apparent errors. And it impedes learning if teachers or students are humiliated, caused to feel guilty if they experiment and fail. In other words, *the most serious error in any system is the suppression of the opportunity to err without condemnation.*

This, of course, does not mean that mistakes should not be corrected. It is the *manner* of correction that is important, the way in which it is learned. I remember, as a little boy, my father asked me what had happened at school, and I said: "I got the closest answer in the class to the question 'How much is twelve times twelve?' I said '142.' " My father was amused, but at any rate closest as I had been I learned my mistake and the correct answer. A sense of humor (but not satire or humiliating laughter) can correct a mistake so that it is learned.

"Don't Blame Me"

"Don't blame me" is a direct response to a fear of being held responsible. It is a defensive hostile reaction to what is perceived to be a hostile accusation by someone with authority, power. To be blamed is to sense a loss of respect and of love. To the recipient of "blame" it is an indication of failure; it is punishing; it arouses guilt feelings, and a loss of power. And so the hostile retort in self-defense: "Don't blame me."

When we do things in a way that parents and teachers disapprove we are "bad." "At the age of five or six the child has acquired an all-pervasive sense of guilt because the conflict between his natural impulses and their moral evaluation by his parents constitutes a constantly generating source of guilt feelings." (Fromm 1947)

Fear of blame is the fear of punishment or degradation. It places a brake on achieving freedom necessary for personal growth, mental health, and enjoyment. The absence of freedom "cripples man and is unhealthy." (Fromm 1973) The fear of blame is the stumbling block that makes recidivists of us, taking us back to the almost powerless period of our early childhood. One of the most frequent reactions is to relieve ourselves of fear by aggression, by defensive behavior to establish a better balance of power, such as going through motions rather than doing the job, timeserving instead of production, following the letter of instructions and withholding initiative. These are typical examples by subordinates of attempts to avoid blame.

One way of saying "Don't blame me" is to put the responsibility for failure on another, as in the famous case of Adam. When the Lord asked him "Did you eat of the tree from which I had forbidden you to eat?" Adam replied, most ungallantly, "The woman You put at my side—she gave me of the tree and I ate." So a child blames another child; a teacher blames a child or advice or directions from someone else.

From the same source we get an example of evasion of responsibility in the form of "Don't blame me. It just happened." When Moses disappeared for forty days and forty nights in a cloud on top of Mount Sinai, the people lost faith in Moses and demanded another god. So Aaron collected their golden jewelry and cast it in a mold and made it into a golden calf. When Moses descended and saw this, he was so angry he broke the tablets, written in the handwriting of the Lord, and asked Aaron to explain. Aaron accused the people of being bent on evil. He admitted collecting the gold and throwing it into the fire and "out came the calf." So we have a common defense— "I'm not responsible. It just happened."

In all ages there have been Adams and Aarons, of both sexes, shedding responsibility for mistakes and rule violations onto others or some undetermined cause or situation when reprimanded by authority. We can also fill in different names and apply these methods to experiences of our own. Try it.

No sense of reality or equity can be developed unless mistakes are admitted, mistakes that society has made and mistakes that the teacher has made, as well as those mistakes that children make. Admission of error makes the correction of mistakes in others less threatening, more bearable and acceptable. The excitement of imagination and curiosity and of fruitful experience of investigative learning must be earthbound by admission of error. Facing one error reduces the chance of further errors. It is also a lesson in humility.

Learning to face mistakes is a surer way to learn reality than to build a redoubt of dogma, of certainty against chance. At every level of organization this requires not endorsement of mistakes but considerable tolerance and supportiveness by higher authorities, persons with greater power.

Underestimating Children

To help children succeed and to enjoy school it is not sufficient to avoid openly calling them failures, thus humiliating them. "We must respect them as thinkers and learners— even when they find school difficult." This does not mean refraining from pointing out mistakes, but rather not doing so in a manner humiliating to children. (Donaldson 1979)

We tend to underestimate the competence of children as thinkers and to overestimate their competence in understanding our language. The language of the school may be different from that spoken in the homes of immigrant parents, and children's understanding of school language may, therefore, present difficulties to them. Black English, a cultural language of many black American youngsters, is rarely comprehensible to teachers. Even the customary usages of words by a teacher may conflict with a child's understanding of the word. Donaldson gives the example of a youngster who explained that he did not like school and would not go back again because the teacher had told him "just sit there for the present" and he had received no present. (Donaldson 1979)

Because young children do not appear to think in our terms we tend to forget that on their own level they are thinking and discriminating. Another young lady I know, not quite two years of age, finished her meal. She had before her a rubber toy, the bowl out of which she had eaten, and her spoon. With a naughty glint in her eyes she picked up the toy and threw it on the floor. She hesitated. She handed the bowl to her grandparents. She hesitated again and kept the spoon which was more personal to herself. It was not action induced by fear—she was merry throughout—it was a thoughtful discrimination and interaction with others.

A three-year-old informed her mother that cats and dogs are animals. Her mother told her that people were too. She thought about this and, as a good biologist differentiating between species, replied, "But people have hands."

Children's experiences being limited they need to have their questions answered if they are to do their own thinking and grow up to be independent, not subservient, people. Independent people, those who wish to participate, members of a democratic society, must be able to ask themselves what they think rather than accept only what the teacher, the boss, the party, a newspaper columnist, or a television commentator thinks for them. Therefore the importance of the curious question and the test of the answer against fact known from experience.

However, as Erich Fromm said, "Students are supposed to learn so many things that they have hardly time and energy left to think. . . . We find today a tremendous enthusiasm for knowledge and education, but at the same time a skeptical or contemptuous attitude toward the allegedly impractical and useless thinking which is concerned 'only' with the truth and which has no exchange value on the market." (Fromm 1947)

Margaret Mead, in discussing the work of an anthropologist in the field, wrote:

> In the field one can take nothing for granted. For as soon as one does, one cannot see what is before one's eyes as fresh and distinctive, and when one treats what is new merely as a variant of something already known, this may lead one far astray. . . . (Mead 1975)

And treatment of the new as merely variants of what is already known is a danger embedded in dogmatic, didactic teaching. Even a teacher's questions can be didactic. And how many times have we seen administrators, supervisors, and school boards dismiss a suggestion because "It was tried before and failed," without consideration of possible human and other environmental variables? No year passed, when I was a member of the New York City Board of Education, that some old-timer did not say that a suggestion for innovation had been tried and failed fifteen or twenty years before, without analysis of why it had failed or in what way.

Controversy and Hypothesis Testing as Learning Tools

When public education gained momentum in the nineteenth century, its pattern, if not always its conscious aim, was to train people to perform obediently in the industrial revolution. Big enterprises did not require inquirers but those who took orders, who performed the menial tasks. Today, however, what is needed from schools is people who can be flexible, who can be creative, who, if they cannot understand what they are doing, are able to inquire. Education needs to build on the instinct of inquiry of little children, their desire to feel their reach, the touch, the taste, and the sound of things, their balance. On this innate instinct of inquiry education should go on to develop the capacity to analyze, select, solve, and behave appropriately to the occasion or problem—to find the adult reach and balance. If education does not do this it is still tuned to the needs of the industrial revolution rather than to a society immersed in technology derived from scientific inquiry.

The 1979–80 National Assessment of Reading and Literature (by the National Assessment of Educational Progress) reported students to have difficulty in explaining in written prose a story or poem. Most students had "a lack of the analytical skills necessary to elaborate, interpret, and defend their views." It was suggested that this was because school curricula favored recitation rather than discussions, resulting in "an emphasis on shallow and superficial opinions at the expense of reasoned and disciplined thought." (*Quarterly Review of Doublespeak* 1982)

This is another example of the unfortunate results of the general failure of schools to permit students and teachers freedom to discuss controversial topics. Controversy need not be hostile. Compared with concurrence seeking and individualistic study, controversy "promotes higher achievement and retention, greater search for information, and more cognitive rehearsal, accurate understanding" etc. (K. Smith et al. 1981)

Controversy was found to promote some uncertainty with respect to the correctness of one's position, a number of subjects switching their opinions to the side which they believed had the strongest arguments. Although it is often presumed that argument leads to hostility and rejection among peers, it was found that in small groups controversy could create greater positive influence on peer relationships by the development of "greater feelings of peer academic support and personal acceptance" than where concurrence was sought. (Smith et al. 1981)

However, it appeared that a few very bright students did better on their own. Such persons are exceptions in many situations, such as in the arts and sciences, for example. But for the generality of persons cooperative discussion of controversial matters without any forced attempt to come to a consensus proved to be the most effective form of education.

The value of controversy is that it gives to the students a sense of alternatives. "[T]here is reason to believe that thought processes themselves are internalizations of social intercourse, an inner colloquy patterned by early external dialogues. It is this that makes education possible. . . . *Education must, then, be not only a transmission of culture but also a provider of alternative views of the world and a strengthener of the will to explore them.*" (Bruner 1961; italics added)

To grow and adapt, to develop from our genesis, we need to learn how to handle controversy. To do so requires an ability to solve problems. The capacity to think, reason, solve problems is not forwarded if learning is limited to information and facts. Such education is for dependence on authority whether the authority of teacher or text—of course, not necessarily valid authority. To learn problem solving, the handling of controversy, necessitate experiencing them in the classroom.

We try to solve problems in two manners: (1) advocacy: how much evidence can be amassed to prove a predetermined conclusion and disprove contrary ones; (2) scientific method: the use of the hypothesis, inquiring whether evidence proves or disproves the hypothesis. Students could be required to write arguments in affirmation and dissent of a proposition and then decide whether and how the hypothesis is correct or not.

This surely will be a more creative and stimulating form of education than the accumulation of the predigested knowledge of the teacher and text. "Over half the population of gifted students do not match their tested ability with comparable achievement in schools." (National Commission on Excellence in Education 1983) Not only the gifted but other students could find stimulation to learning by introducing them in early grades to a scientific mode of thinking. This might well encourage their entry into the sciences—our need today—as well as assist them in problem solving and handling controversy.

This is not offered merely as a teaching technique. Above all it is a method to increase the students' ability to meet new situations, to solve their problems, to increase their sense of social power and thus reduce hostility and a need to counterattack.

Human Relations vs. Interaction

From infancy we have to relate to other people and our environment. A difficulty with the general conception of human *relations* is that it is immobile, like a statue or a picture, although probably less stimulating to the imagination. To speak of a teacher-student relationship (or a teacher-supervisor relationship) is inadequate. This is a static concept. In reality there are teacher-student (or teacher-supervisor) *interactions* or *transactions* in which each person interacts with the other. Each has a series and variety of transactions with the other. The whole universe testifies to the fact that there can be no existence without an interactive relationship with other things, from galaxies to the food chain. We *transact* with other persons positively or by avoidance behavior. It is interactive behavior that determines what and who one is. As Gerard Manley Hopkins put it: "What I do is me: for that I came." (Hopkins 1963)

These interactions and transactions are never still. They involve new positions, new estimates, and a variety of understandings and misunderstandings. "A relationship with no combat in it is dull, and a relationship with too much combat in it is toxic. What is desirable is a relationship with a certain optimum of conflict." (Bateson 1979) In other words a certain tension can be a plus. This cannot be where dogma prevails, for the tension then will tend to be hostile or submissive, that is, negative. The golden rule expresses a measure, a positive measure, of interaction, not a relationship.

Cultures and Discrimination

"Toxic" combat, extremely hostile combat, frequently occurs between the school and children of what may to some be considered pariah cultures, cultures of blacks, Latin Americans and, except perhaps Chinese and Japanese, non-European stocks, children of the very poor, children of the slums. We tend to regard these people as lower caste, as unequal until they reach upper-middle-class status and then, often reluctantly, they are received. The children of these cultures learn young the lesson of unacceptability. Countee Cullen's poem of the little eight-year-old black boy in the trolley car is a model. He saw a little white boy, also about eight, looking at him and evidently felt a kinship:

> And so I smiled, but he poked out
> His tongue, and called me, "Nigger."
> (Cullen 1927)

And that was all that he remembered of his trip to Baltimore.

To go to school with the expectations of increasing power and opportunity and feeling a capacity to achieve and then to find one is unacceptable, or less acceptable than others, will inevitably result in feeling comparative deprivation and arouse hostility. There are other sources of comparative deprivation for children of the slums. They begin life with fewer cultural advantages than middle-class children, such as books and art in the home, and conversation on broad nonpersonal topics, the kind of experience that makes more comprehensible the symbolic learning that is a major factor in school education.

Teachers, like the rest of us who are middle-class or are ardently engaged in rising from lower economic origins, have rare social contacts with slum people whatever their race. This is especially true of whites, although tribalism knows no racial or national origin in its conscious or unconscious bigotry. There is no love lost between American blacks and blacks from the Caribbean, or among immigrants from Cuba, Mexico, and Jamaica. Every group wants to be regarded as superior to some even lower caste. "We do not know them. They are not our kind." And so we tend not to respect their subcultures which tend at points to clash, at least not to mesh, with the dominant culture that schools feel it is their mission to teach. (This reminds me that once in a class of graduate students I used the sociologic term "subcultures" in relation to Harlem and other black communities and was upbraided by one of my black students for belittling black culture by the use of the term "sub.")

It is the rare missionary, seated behind the desk—that bastion between the wielder of power and the dependents—who can understand or respect the cultures in which many children of slums are participants. In addition to the normal lack of social power children feel in class, these children are cursed by the reality of deprivation of social power *as* a class. Disorder and violence are commonplace in black ghettos and barrios. These are the hostile responses common to those who have little or no intellectual, political, or economic power. Words and reasoned discussions lack the efficacy of machismo. So disorder and violence are frequently their manner of attempting to establish a balance of power or power dominance in the inner city schools.

Truants and Dropouts

Most of us have at some time played hookey or absented ourselves from classes. We derived a certain delight in this sinfulness. It gave us a sense of adjusting the balance of social power. Truancy and dropping-out, however, are different. They are symptoms of hostility. They are outright rejections.

Truancy and dropping-out can only be reduced if schools are made more interesting, more acceptable, less threatening, more competitive to the freedom and lack of responsibility of the street, poolroom, movies, TV, and gang. (With respect to gangs, it has been suggested that rather than being a cause of delinquent behavior, having delinquent friends "is more likely a consequence of needing support for one's own delinquent behavior.") (Gold and Mann 1982)

To make schools as appealing as the outside, to reduce the number of dropouts and truants, would not be achieved by extending school time as proposed in *A Nation at Risk* (National Commission on Excellence in Education 1983) because it would not touch those most in need. More school time to those most at risk would mean more days and hours of frustration, more reduction of their sense of power. They are already discouraged and failing. Most truants and dropouts say they are "not interested in school." (Marriage and pregnancy are the reasons most frequently given by young women for dropping-out.) (Boyer 1983)

We must be careful not to blame them until we have analyzed why school is a waste of time to them, why it is neither interesting nor supportive, what has happened to their sense of social power, and to what extent do schools contribute to this.

How can we give to these young people a sense that learning and excellence are of value to them? The Carnegie Study found that a variety of special programs has been developed for "disadvantaged students" and that "at the heart of every effort that appeared to be succeeding, we noticed that there was a close relationship between a student and a counselor or teacher—there was a mentor with high standards and clear goals, one who had gained the student's confidence and trust." They, therefore, recommended the development of programs for high-risk students with "special tutoring and a supportive relationship between a teacher and each student." (Boyer 1983; Gold 1978) A lecture about values is unlikely to help. It must be learned by experience, through support, with some hope for a future, and the rewards of security.

A Nation at Risk emphasized the responsibility of parents; but the parents of many of the youngsters most at risk have little sense of responsibility for their children's education or little time or energy to give to their children, to supervise homework, for example. They, themselves, usually lack the educational and the cultural background of the parents of children who are more successful in the school. Their homes are in most instances without books. Their TV programs range from soap operas to dramas of violence. Their music is limited to the current popular mode. For the most part truants and dropouts "have more siblings, more broken homes, higher levels of parental punitiveness, and lower self-esteem. . . . Simply put, many students who leave school come from stressful homes." (Boyer 1983)

The values of many students are far from the values of educators. An example, perhaps an extreme one, is an occurrence at Yonkers (New York) High School. There the superintendent had transferred a football coach to a teaching assignment at another high school because he had allowed a student to play football without a proper physical examination and without a signed permission slip from the student's parents, and the student had died as a result of playing football. The students protested the transfer and surrounded the car of the superintendent and refused to let her leave. Evidently to the students, a successful football team ranked higher than life and death. Sports above all else. (*The New York Times*, October 20, 1983)

Many young people are attracted to extracurricular activities other than sports. These have holding power for them. Perhaps we give too little attention to such school activities. Why should there generally be a gap between what is learned in them and what is required in the classroom? Extracurricular activities are not compulsory, of course, and they contribute to the interests of those who participate, answer *their* questions, and are not autocratic. Possibly we should study in depth why extracurricular activities have a holding power the normal curriculum fails to provide.

As holding a job appears to stabilize many young people, the holding power of a school may be increased by work-study programs. These are hard to develop without the active participation of business and labor. But this has and can be done. (Boyer 1983)

Hostility may be directed against the self, as in the case of drug abuse. Poverty, discrimination, and social disorder contribute to this; but these young people also have a sense of personal failure, rejection, and low esteem. They lack hope and they have distrust and fear of others. (Chein et al. 1964)

For schools to be of help to high-risk students it is necessary that they have programs, possibly alternate programs, that will impress the students with their fairness and flexibility. The curricula must meet the level and pace of the students and the style of teaching should "convey a sense of personal caring and support." (Gold and Mann 1982) This is far different than a confrontational style or the requirement that these students, who find little interest, support, or sense of achievement, must perform as more normal students do to meet standards required of more ordinary students. In other words we are talking about school situations that raise students' sense of social power and reduce a sense of failure, and disinterest, and antagonism to learning.

But always, always, a goal should be to enable those students who receive special or alternate forms of education to return to normal classrooms, participating in their work without disruptive behavior. It isn't easy.

On the whole teachers have not the freedom, the experience, or (often understandably) the fortitude to solve the school problems of these children. Teachers whose professional techniques are in words and symbols find themselves unable, usually, to handle violence or the threat of violence except on a win-lose basis. Their freedom to solve such problems is hampered by the public and leaders in school systems who tend to move toward punishment or other win-lose solutions, a shape-up or else, a confrontation method of solution. We treat symptoms without searching for causes, especially causes in our own behavior that might exacerbate a situation.

6 Teachers Also Have Shackles

You cannot teach a man anything; you can only help him to find it within himself.

—Galileo

It is true of teachers, as of children, that if they have not freedom to use imagination and initiative, they will not feel secure, and they will tend to counterattack. They require freedom to perform in a professional manner. There is complaint about the quality of teachers. There are unquestionably a number of causes for this when in fact their inadequacy exists. May not a frequent cause be that they are so often frustrated and made hostile by an entrapment in a bureaucracy or because more self-secure and independent-minded people will not teach under the frequent petty tyrannies of supervisors or dictates of the local citizenry?

For all the sympathy one must have for children controlled by a bureaucracy and however disturbing the hostility that is stimulated in them by school, there must also be sympathy for teachers and supervisors. Their life space in their profession is fenced by barbs. Their freedom is generally restricted. They are told the line to follow. Of course there must be standards of instruction. Teachers like students will flounder without them, will not know what is expected of them. But must standards be imposed?

One can be disappointed by teachers, sometimes outraged by them. They are often justly criticized for incompetence, unfairness, and lack of motivation. But like the children in their classes they may be shackled by authority and denied opportunities to be imaginative. One supposed misstep may result in the pillory of teachers or administrators and a thousand, sensible, sound actions ignored. This is so in large organizations of inner-city schools when relations among them, parents, and school authorities tend to be impersonal, as well as in small communities in which everybody's complaint can echo down every street.

If a standard (that the teachers had little or no part in setting) has been unmet, retribution is threatening. The power of the hierarchy generally corrupts by its usages: by reduction of initiative in subordinates, by cultivating unwillingness to take the risks of creativity, by displacing responsibility for results with obedience, submission to authority, and by reduction of satisfactions and a sense of social power. The inevitable result is hostility which may be directed upward or downward in the hierarchy. Downward is safer.

> Threat induces defensiveness and reduces both the tolerance of ambiguity and the openness to the new and unfamiliar; excessive tension leads to a primitivization and a stereotyping of thought-processes. As Rokeach has pointed out, *threat and excessive tension lead to the closed rather than open mind.* (Deutsch 1973; italics added)

A chain of power begins with a school board and descends through the superintendent to the principal, the teacher, and finally the student. At each level the power becomes weaker and more dependent on a higher rank. There is a footnote to this, however: administrative personnel frequently have longer terms of office than school board members and are able to ignore the board. And in large school districts principals often can perform their tasks as they believe proper without their supervisors' awareness. I have seen this occur a number of times in New York City schools. Many an orchid grows in a crack.

Some Teacher Problems

Rutter et al. (1979) reassert what has been common knowledge for centuries, that because schooling is compulsory, the fact that children *have* to attend in itself may make for tensions and antagonisms. They cite Gordon (1957) to the effect that "the force of the informal student subculture" stands in opposition to educational ideology; and to Sugarman (1967) who found that the culture of youth "was linked with a thoroughgoing alienation from school." Thus there may be a contest for control and this may be an extension of more general social conflicts. Unwittingly teachers and their students may be impelled to act out dramas originating beyond the school walls.

Imaginative learning is so often under wraps because imaginative teaching may be proscribed. There is the recent case of a teacher in Maryland who, in the course of teaching *Julius Caesar*, gave his students some material from Aristotle's *Poetics* and Machiavelli's *The Prince*, to illuminate the political concepts of Shakespeare's play. He was suspended for this departure from tradition.

Two explanations were given for this reaction: a school board member said, "We have the responsibility for having the same kind of education available to every child." And the school superintendent suggested that "[I]n a public school system, you have to have reasonable procedures to determine what is to be used and the superintendent has to uphold them." He was worried that if teachers had freedom they might introduce magazines such as *Playboy* to the class. (Hechinger November 4, 1980)

If school administrators cannot distinguish between Aristotle and Machiavelli on the one hand and sexist magazines on the other, how are teachers to be encouraged to expand the cultural experiences of students? How can they themselves avoid frustration? And a sense of loss of power?

In most schools the course of study and the text, in the creation or adoption of which teachers rarely have much choice, become the intellectual authorities. The official ritual is to hold to them and follow them. This may offer security to teachers and avoid threatening encounters with those higher in the hierarchy—the typical pattern of bureaucracy. But it prevents a good learning situation in which inquiry and imagination may flourish. It stunts students and teachers.

Textbooks

Among the burdens teachers carry are many of the textbooks imposed on them. Seventeen states have centralized textbook selection. They place teachers and students in a monolithic intellectual environment. Teachers have little individual choice. Statewide adoptions are remote from the classroom. Even systemwide teacher adoption committees tend to deprive teachers of initiative. There appears to be fear—often justified—that teachers might use bigoted, radical, or otherwise distorted teaching materials. So textbook selection is "protective," in effect, is a form of censorship. Might not teachers have a greater sense of power and inducement to initiative if the choice of teaching materials were left to the faculty of each school? The fear of increased cost of multiple choices and of removing controls and thus by this provide the opportunity to make "mistakes" will limit such a sensible arrangement. Meanwhile, we shall have prettily packaged books.

The National Commission on Excellence in Education report points out that there are too few experienced teachers and scholars who are involved in writing textbooks. Textbooks are written down by their publishers to ensure statewide adoptions and thus increase the market. The report refers to a study that revealed that "a majority of students were able to master 80% of the material in some of their subject-matter text before they had even opened the books. Many books do not challenge the students to whom they are assigned." (1983)

Textbook publishing houses do considerable research concerning the appropriateness of the texts for the ages of their audiences. However, profit is the goal and acceptability by state education departments and schools may override educational values. An example of this is the revision of science textbooks to ensure that they do not offend believers in "creationism" (based largely on the belief that the opening chapters of the Book of Genesis account for creation) and thus not interfere with sales. In some texts the discussion of Darwinism has been reduced. Teachers may, therefore, be constrained by texts that are tempered by current or local popular notions and prejudices.

Textbook selection has stimulated attempts at censorship. In a case in Texas some self-appointed censors objected to a story containing the question "How could they sing of the land of the free when there was still racial discrimination?" The censors denied this, declaring that the majority of people are free and only those in jail are not free.

There have been many instances of disputes concerning selection of school texts and library books, the failure to select them, and their removal from classrooms and library shelves. There have been cases involving the use of teaching materials that had not been specifically approved by boards of education. Court actions have been brought by teachers, students, parents, and school boards. Struggles concerning books and other teaching materials have aroused some of the most vicious attacks on schools and teachers.

The most frequent source of conflict has been the legal rights and powers of boards of education representing the public, that is, the majority of local populations, as against the rights of students to information and teachers to free speech. The courts have been in conflict as to the breadth of the application of the guarantee of the First Amendment of freedom of speech. "While the public schools are not constitutionally prohibited from espousing particular viewpoints or from engaging in social and civil indoctrination, they may not transgress the Constitution's limits on infringement of free speech and expression. It seems clear that the states themselves may not determine where those limits lie; that responsibility must rest with the courts." (Estreicher 1980) And courts have frequently indicated to school boards the limits of their powers under the Constitution. (*Thomas v. Board of Education* 1979)

Under the First Amendment students' rights are violated when a board of education orders the removal of books from library shelves which it characterizes as "anti-American, anti-Christian, anti-Semitic, and just plain filthy." The Supreme Court has held that while local school boards may have broad discretion in their management of school affairs, this discretion must be exercised "in a manner that comports with the transcendent imperatives of the First Amendment. Students do not 'shed their rights to freedom of speech or expression at the schoolhouse gate.' " The removal of books may affect such rights. "Local school boards may not remove books from school libraries simply because they dislike the ideas contained in those books and seek by their removal to 'prescribe what shall be orthodox in politics, nationalism, religion, or other matters of opinion.' " (*Board of Education, Island Trees Union Free School District v. Pico* 1982; *Tinker v. Des Moines School District* 1969)

"In our system, students may not be regarded as closed-circuit recipients of only that which the State chooses to communicate." (*Tinker v. Des Moines School District* 1969)

Relation to Students

Many teachers, as indeed most adults, regard themselves not merely as having greater experience and more accurate perceptions than children, but also as being superior to them. We adults frequently cannot quite consider children as persons in their own right, as equals, living in a "state of availability . . . not yet anything determinate and irrevocable, . . . " (Ortega y Gasset 1956.)

There are teachers who regard children as necessary nuisances, whose nurture is a way to earn a living, little more.

They teach without being fond of teaching. Their emotional satisfactions will then be from the power they have in the classroom. However, there are also many teachers who regard nurturing as their calling, who satisfy their own needs by helping children develop their capacities, share in their hopes, and want to assist the young to avoid their own mistakes.

> Be spared! Here, here take of my wisdom won,
> These are the very rocks I fell upon.
>   (L. Marshall 1969)

What does the teacher require of students? Dorwin Cartwright (1966) refers to a study of a teacher's power over students. Seventy-three percent of the teachers regard as important the student "being respectful" and "accepting the teacher as authority." Forty-two percent referred to "obedience." These, of course, are the needs of authorities. When pupils increase their force, the teacher must change tactics or have a hostile confrontation. In large classes the teacher will tend to become more authoritarian, more didactic and dogmatic and less able to treat students as individuals. This, of course, will tend to be felt as less respect and as a loss of social power by the students.

Often teachers are oversensitive to the likes or dislikes and possible criticism of their students. As others who have low self-esteem in a power-laden situation that provides little or no support for them, they may see a situation as threatening. They will perceive the exercise of power, of control over goal attainment as a threat to self-esteem, a lessening of social power. They, therefore, must emphasize respect and obedience to reinforce their self-esteem.

Except when they have passed the age of compulsory education children are captive audiences. Teachers, too, may feel trapped in the hierarchy of their profession, especially after achieving tenure and some retirement rights. Having taught their captive audiences for years they may be unprepared to perform other work or for the competitiveness of the marketplace. That is why it is important to involve teachers in planning because this may be seen as a sharing of power.

For there is an almost universal need to feel oneself as a contributor, as accomplishing something meaningful, to do a good job, and to receive recognition for it. As has been said of other workers, "They do feel a need, however, and they do appreciate, having a voice in deciding those issues closely related to their own work lives." (Bowers 1977) The opportunity for teachers to participate in planning for change is not ordinarily under their control but under that of the central administrative staff, the board of education, and the funding agency. (Firestone 1977) This will be elaborated in the following chapters.

Because of their own needs teachers are reluctant to share power with their students, for the dependency of students can be supportive of the self-image of teachers. This inability of most teachers to share power in the classroom, because they require supportiveness from pupil dependency as recompense for their own dependence on supervisors and school boards, carries a penalty. It interferes with the maturity of teachers. This is apparent in Bel Kaufman's *Up the Down Staircase* (1965).

Contradictory Adult Demands

Contradictory values and relationships between adults have detrimental effects on children. The experience of Augustine is relevant. Clark and Van Sommers (1961) in their study of the relation of children's behavior to adults who are in conflict found that these unsatisfactory relationships were accompanied by adult-child relationships that were also unsatisfactory. Basic to this is the child's exposure "to contradictory demands for allegiance and other behavior by the adults who were in conflict." Such contradictory demands were also found to be related to maladjusted behavior at school "where attitude, achievement, conduct, peer relations, sporting ability, and attendance were affected."

Contradictory adult demands, they found, "were associated with a child being difficult to control by adults." This would indicate that some of the behavioral difficulties of children in schools originated in home conflict between parents or parents and grandparents. (Such conflict between demands—and values—can be accentuated for children of broken homes when both parents share custody or a parent has visitation rights.) This finding is also relevant to interaction between teachers and parents and the importance of harmonizing them. One of the findings of Clark and Sommers is that in the order of allegiance in cases of adult conflict, the mother tends to come first, the father second, and other adults third. Thus we can assume that in a conflict between the precepts or norms of parents and teachers the child will be likely to side with those of the parents. There appear to be no studies of the effects of contrary demands by teachers and supervisors.

We may assume that if the home has little expectation that education will result in economic benefit, this will influence a child's initiative and perspective. (Myrdal 1963) This will pose a hurdle to a teacher attempting to reach and stimulate the child. If there is a conflict between the culture and expectations of a family and the mores and expectations of the school— perhaps between the subculture of the family and the prevailing national culture—there is a strong possibility of conflict between teachers and students. In an era of reversion to worldwide tribalism (as ours appears to be) such conflicts are to be expected and can only be ameliorated by understanding, respect, and compromise. They are exacerbated if schools by word or attitude denigrate foreign subcultures. Certainly punishment is not an effective solution. Development of school-home relations needs priority. But here again the life-space of the teacher may be hampered by the anxiety and hostility inherent in bureaucracy. And teachers in inner-city schools may with reason fear to visit the homes of students.

Expectations, Labeling, and Grading

Labeling can become a self-fulfilling prophecy. Our behavior and performance are affected by what we perceive others to expect of us and they expect our behavior and performance to conform to their expectations. Rosenthal and Jacobson (1968) found that where teachers were informed that certain children were highly competent and others low in capacity, they tended to mark the former higher and the latter lower even though, in fact, the information was incorrect.

While Rutter et al. (1979) has some objections to the findings of Rosenthal and Jacobson, they cite another study to the effect that "pupils taught by the same teachers as their older siblings had higher academic attainments than pupils taught by different teachers if their older siblings had been academically bright but lower achievements if their siblings had been dull." (Seaver 1973) They refer to other studies which indicated that the expectations and attitudes of teachers do have an impact on the manner in which they behave toward their pupils. (They add the caveat that, of course, not all teachers may respond in the same manner.)

Children react to teachers in a similar way. In an experiment in a school setting one teacher gave solvable problems to a fifth-grade class and another gave unsolvable problems. When the second teacher—who had given the unsolvable problems—later presented the class with the identical problems they had been able to solve for the first teacher, they were unable to solve them. (Dweck and Reppucci 1973) This was described as "learned helplessness." It may be comparable to the findings in the Lewin, Lippitt, and White study (described in chapter 1) that children were slow to adapt to a democratic after having been in an autocratic atmosphere.

For various reasons school officials have traditionally made assumptions concerning attitude, habits, and talents children have brought with them to the classroom. In general teachers have believed that children who come from prosperous, stable families would do better than those from poor, unstable families.

Tests, too, may be founded on assumptions concerning student achievement.

> . . . There were always some exceptions to that general rule, but both research findings and conventional wisdom

supported these beliefs about student achievement measured in the conventional ways—teacher-made tests, standardized tests, and course grades. The job of the teacher and
the school was to move the children into the curriculum,
which was also organized along these assumptions. This
pattern is found not just in the United States but to a considerable degree in every other nation with a well-defined educational system. (Graham in *Daedalus*, 1980)

Deutsch suggests that because fellow students tend to have
more full and detailed knowledge of each other than the
teacher, but the teacher usually has more expert experience and
judgment, there might be joint responsibility in grading. (This
suggestion deserves experimental research.) Such a format, of
course, would require a cooperative relationship. However, "a
grading system which is completely controlled by the teachers
helps to enhance the teacher's power vis-a-vis the students and
buttress his superordinate position." (Deutsch 1979)

He goes on to say that " . . . So far as I know, there is no good
research evidence which would suggest that the learning of students is inferior if they are not in a subordinate relation to their
teachers." Can they ever not be subordinate? To what extent can
they be equals, partners? If not, the next question is: to what
extent can the climate of a classroom be such that the teacher as
leader does not bring insubordination out of subordination?

Often, as we know, in order to avoid trouble with students or
their parents, grades are sometimes inflated, thus destroying
the value of the grade. The same has been true of advancing
students year by year even though they have failed to meet the
standards of the grade. To the student this must inevitably indicate that little is expected of him or her, depreciate the concept
of quality performance, and reduce incentive.

The old theory that the IQ was irreversible no longer holds.
The IQs of students who have repeatedly failed tend to decline
and those who are encouraged tend to rise. The judgment of
examiners, in other words, is imperfect. The experience of Einstein, who was denied admittance to the Polytechnic Institute
in Zurich, is one example. Verdi was refused admittance to the

Conservatory of Music in Milan because he did not show sufficient devotion to music.

The story already told of the girl who would not volunteer in class because she disagreed with the teacher but gave the teacher what she wanted on examinations is relevant to the marking system. Some degree of conformity to the views and values of the grading authority in general appears necessary to obtain high marks. "[A]lthough a creative personal reorientation in a student may enhance his growth in cognitive capabilities and academic learning, it leads to a relative deprivation in the grades he receives." (Boyle 1969) Once again we face the submergence of imagination and creativity by ritually imposed standards.

Tests

To achieve success in a test is another inducement to do what teachers want. Answers marked "correct" tend to indicate "children's knowledge about what the 'society' expects of them, rather than their knowledge about the reality they know, or the way in which they think through problems." Meier (1981) gives examples of test answers that accord better with the mature expression of adults rather than with that of youngsters. For instance, look at the following reading test questions and the answers deemed to be correct:

> Some days I should stay in bed. Today was one of those days.
> "Good morning," Mom said. "Don't you have a clean shirt to wear? That one looks dirty."
> "Sam," said Dad, "your shoes are on the wrong feet."
> I got dressed all over again. By the time I ate breakfast, my cereal was soggy. Then I stopped, as usual, for Bill. He was not home. He had already gone to school. I walked there alone.
> When I got to school, Bill yelled, "Here comes Sam, the snail."

> Why was Sam so slow in getting to school?
> He overslept.

He had to get dressed twice.
He fooled around.
He did not like school.

Most of the children with whom this question was discussed said "Sam was fooling around." A few children said "He probably didn't like school; that's why he was fooling around and his friends called him a snail." The correct answer is: He had to get dressed twice.

Another question asks children to select the proper ending to the sentence:

An architect's most important tools are his—

(E) pencil and paper
(F) buildings
(G) ideas
(H) bricks

Most children selected (E) pencil and paper. Was it "reading ability" or something else that led others to the "right" answer, (G) ideas?

Another example:

A giant is always   (E) huge   (F) fierce   (G) mean
(H) scary

The correct answer is huge. But if children pick scary, does that mean they are "wrong" or that they can't read huge, fierce, or mean? or giant?

In summary, Meier says: "But since 'good reading' requires knowledge about the world, a narrow focus on testing 'skills' deprives children of the substance of literacy in a quest for good scores." (Meier 1981)

And high scores give no indication that the student has learned how to handle new problems.

These questions and the proper answers demanded indicate again the mistake we adults so frequently make when assuming that children's world is our world. What they get from reading and what we get from reading are closely tied to our respective experiences and our respective values.

If students may be frustrated by tests and angered by failure, teachers may also find frustration and become angered by the tests they are required to give and the preparation of classes to pass them. Lydia Simmons, a New York high-school teacher, told of a girl who could read a passage perfectly but did not "know," did not comprehend what she had read. Because the student was able to read the passage, the teacher did not realize the student could not read with understanding.

> I feel I should have realized she couldn't read. That I
> didn't is due to the fact that I "taught to the test," spending
> most of my time preparing students for their competency
> exams and giving little attention to literature.

She and some of her fellow teachers had come to realize that the annual reading tests that become "a political issue when the results are published" were more harmful than they were helpful for "they gear kids to pass tests rather than to think. Scores, finally, become all that is important. Learning is beside the point." (Simmons 1981)

Although they may not indicate the reasons for success or failure, some kind of tests may be necessary tools to check the success or failure of teaching. More important are tests that can be used to understand students, their needs and problems. (And teachers frequently do devise such tests—examiners rarely do.) Whether what is learned can be applied, utilized, is the proper goal of education not recall. Mechanically arrived at test scores must fail to determine this.

However, if tests are tuned to the decibels of the adults who devise them rather than to those of the students who take them, or if their passing becomes the goal of the classroom rather than learning, it is the tests themselves that fail and do not pass, not the students or their teachers. Yet, students and teachers and their schools are generally blamed for low scores and for the ignorance of high-school graduates. Reliance on standard test scores may be diversionary. The more serious failures may result from the battlefield of the classroom.

In conclusion we may summarize by saying that the grading system may be a frustrating puzzle to teachers. It also may be a cause of hostility in students who regard the questions or required answers to be unfair or low marks as a punishment, as a form of comparative deprivation. Standardized tests may not be relevant as indicators of ability or knowledge, while preparation to pass them may distract teachers and students from learning and imaginative expression.

Discipline and Punishment

Misbehavior and delinquency, like crime, are labels. As Bateson (1979) stated, crime "is the name of a way of organizing actions. It is therefore unlikely that punishing the act will extinguish the crime." The labels are not realities. They are static and as such provide no understanding of the dynamic conditions causing the labeled behavior. Again it can be said, as in the case of "violence" (Blumenthal et al. 1972), interpretations of the terms "misbehavior" and "delinquency" will vary with the cultural and life experiences of the definer, his or her economic and educational status, and the extent of threat that particular behavior provokes.

Aggressiveness of a delinquent should not be considered as mere protest against restrictions or living conditions. Nor is it necessarily exuberance, or getting even, or showing off. It may be the result of "elemental recognition that power can be achieved only by cutting loose from the power systems established by others, and by setting up, arbitrarily or capriciously, a limited power system of one's own." (Murphy 1947) Even infants howl (or laugh) to get what they want—food, attention—a first exercise in power over parents.

It is the relationships, or better, the interactions that need to be analyzed before labeling behavior. Aggression, dependency, hostility, pride, misbehavior, and delinquency, "[a]ll such words have their roots in what happens between persons, not in some something-or-other inside a person." (Bateson 1979) This is also true of the words discipline and punishment.

Rutter et al. (1979) make a distinction between discipline and punishment. They cite a finding that a combination of good discipline (rule enforcement), involvement of pupils in discipline, and little use of corporal punishment was in most cases associated with good attendance. Hostility is a more likely ingredient of punishment than of discipline.

Making the punishment fit the crime is simpler than making it fit the criminal or the disruptive or rambunctious child. In Mosaic law it was a hand for a hand. In Arabic law, chopping off the right hand, in addition to the resulting pain and physical disability, made the felon unacceptable as a dinner companion because only the right hand may be used for eating out of the common dish. Dismissal from school may fit the "crime," remove a disrupter from the classroom; it, too, in effect, exiles the offender. But after all, the fitness of the punishment is subjective. The effects are not necessarily so. Judge Bazelon (1970) advises that:

> . . . The school will have to learn how to work out disputes between teachers and pupils, without turning the troublemakers over to some other agency. It must above all not let go of the youngster, no matter how irritating and upsetting he is. It must not lose him to the streets.

It used to be common practice to discipline students by requiring them to come early or to remain after school to repeat or do extra work. This comparatively mild but effective form of discipline is not usually feasible today when, for example, children are brought to school and returned home by bus. Nor can this system be utilized where teacher contracts forbid prolonging the school day before or beyond certain hours.

As mentioned in chapter 1 the Vera Institute of Justice found that delinquents and other school dropouts did well in storefront academies that were better able than the more rigid school systems to adapt to their needs, to respect them and their capacities. And dropping out of regular school "decreased the probability of further delinquency."

Some schools may contribute to delinquency by remaining passive in the face of children's problems, and they may actively encourage delinquency "by the use of methods that create the conditions of failure for certain students." A former director of youth services in Florida states, "I used to blame delinquency on parents and schools about fifty fifty. Now I blame the schools for 85% of it." (Strasburg 1978)

Rutter et al. cite Heal (1978) whose findings were to the effect that in schools with formal punishment systems misbehavior was the worst, and Clegg and Megson (1968) that in schools with a great deal of corporal punishment, delinquency rates tended to be highest. The countereffectiveness of punishments may be largely the result of their retributive character, retribution stimulating or enhancing hostility, counterattack.

Standards and firmness, however, must be distinguished from punishment. To receive a good mark, promotion to another grade, or a school diploma, a student must be held to a good attendance record and must do the work that has to be done. Otherwise there will be no education in schools, no social education, no sense of responsibility developed, and a laissez-faire or permissive situation will be created that can only result in frustration and hostility. Insistence on standards for advancement or a diploma need not be done as punishment—though some may interpret it as such.

Confrontations are always emotionally charged. This leads to win-lose situations, intensifying differences, distorting perceptions, and increasing resistance to attempts to change behavior. Supportive behavior can lead to a win-win situation because thought processes are not distorted by antagonistic emotional forces.

Such supportive behavior is often difficult for teachers, sometimes because of temperament, sometimes because of insecurity, sometimes because of classroom tension (which may be of their own doing), and probably just as often because they feel threatened by the expectations of superiors and others. Except for young children no one wants to be "treated as a child"—children by teachers and teachers by supervisors. Disparagement or an indignity may reduce students and teachers to tears, in fact or figuratively. As Kunitz warned, "Observe that tears are bullets when they harden." (Kunitz 1979)

Student and teacher have the capacity to punish each other, to practice retribution. They probably identify with different kinds of people, have to some extent different values, and consequently may engage in retributive conduct in opposition to the other's values—thus the classroom battlefield.

Support from peer groups increases aggressive reactions toward a power figure and reduces acceptance of the person and ideas of such figure. "Without the support of the peer groups, the individual accepts the power figure much more as a person." And it has been experimentally shown that subordinates in their private evaluations of supervisors' behavior tended to attribute more cooperativeness and reasonableness to them than they did as members of a group. (Stotland 1966)

Peer group support sustains teachers as well as students. Mutual supportiveness of the teaching staff affects the atmosphere, the ethos of a school, including attitudes toward discipline and punishment. Supportiveness from other teachers is less likely to occur when each teacher is isolated in his or her classroom, consultation with each other is difficult, and joint consideration of problems not promoted by the principal.

We are not only what we think we are but also what others believe we are. It is the interactions of these roles and their respective valences that determine our behavior in society. Is punishment a response to the behavior that the punished person believes to be appropriate to his or her self-image or to his or her failure to satisfy the expectations of others? Failure can be seen as a penalty and is often associated with delinquency. Grades and class standing are indices to students of the teacher's evaluation of them. If they feel that the probability is that they will fail or that they are not likely to gain passing marks, students may find few advantages in continued participation in school where success is judged by marks. The mark "failed" may not be punitive. Nevertheless it may be perceived as such, or at least as making effort not worthwhile. This does not imply that the failed ought to be passed. Rather it should prompt inquiry as to the personal interactions as well as the other causes of failures, the blocks to success and how they may be mediated. This may be too difficult for many teachers and school systems, or if they are willing to accept the responsibility they might lack the financial means adequately to assay each student failure.

William James's analogy of the classroom to a battlefield is in part the result of teachers feeling handicapped by a loss of social power and a lack of professional space. Job security and adequate income are not enough. These alone do not give security. To a greater or lesser degree, therefore, teachers are under tension. Few people who have not taught appreciate the stresses of teaching.* "In effect, excessive tension reduces the intellectual resources available for discovering new ways of coping with a problem or new ideas for resolving a conflict." (Deutsch 1973)

*Every layman should read the excellent description of the day-to-day work load of a good teacher, typical if not universal, in Sizer (1984, p. 14).

7 Who's in Charge

Statutory and Other Limitations

It has been said that a board of education has discretion in spending only about 20 percent of its budget. "While the accuracy of these percentages might be questioned, there can be no doubt that mandated programs determined the expenditure of the major part of public school budgets." (Connery 1978) Connery continues: "Although a school board still had a fifth of the budget to spend as it chose even the responsibility for these expenditures sometimes could be shifted to the federal or state governments or the teachers' union."

The states have imposed on education "a numbing hodge-podge of rules and regulations." For example, the California education code fills four volumes and 3700 pages; New York State's education law is in five volumes and 5000 pages. Can all these words help or must they confuse? (Boyer 1983)

Ever since our nation began—until the last two decades—education with few exceptions was a concern of the states. It was a function of states, their responsibility. The states distributed this responsibility among thousands of local school boards and provided that the schools should be for the most part locally financed. There has now been a change in the emphasis of the law from requirements to provide *equal opportunity* (whether separate or not) to *equal education*. To bring this about the federal government, as well as the states, provided considerable financing. (Graham 1980) Especially since the desegregation movement began in 1956, many school districts have not had sufficient experts to readapt educational programs as they concern community relations and requirements. Almost all school districts have been confused. To each new program financed, the federal government attached rules for implementation and reporting, as, for example, by Title 1 (new Chapter 1) of the Elementary and Secondary School Act. More and more, therefore, he who paid the piper called the tune. And not only the tune changed to confuse teachers but often its pitch and tempo.

This shift in support and responsibility for education was to a great extent brought about by the failure of schools to give equal education (and even equal opportunity for education) to children of different races and economic conditions. Equal opportunity was frequently equated to a seat for every child and twelve years of schooling. The child handicapped, whether because of intellectual or physical disability, or by being from the "underclass" of poverty, of the deprived, was not treated equally compared with "normal children." The child who was brought from another country, speaking some language other than English at home, was left to blunder along as best he or she could. In many school systems there were and are not now even language vestibule classes; and the doors from the vestibules, although perhaps not locked, are often closed. As in other situations in life the weaker are expected to adapt, not the stronger. It was the successful (for generations the white, Anglo-Saxon Protestants) who were paying for and calling the tune, the tune they believed had been good for them and so must be for all others. If the others did not like the tune, so much the worse for them. Do we not expect others to do as we do and accept what we accept at the same time that, paradoxically, we regard and treat them as different?

Since the Supreme Court decision in 1954, in *Brown v. Board of Education,* there was not merely some relocation of school populations but a change in educational ethics which many were unready to and others would not accept. Change was commanded and educators and parents were unprepared. They did not understand what was happening, nor did they understand what the imposed changes expected of them. They felt "whipsawed, disaffected, and *even* resentful." (Atkin 1980; italics added) Values that are imposed rarely seem to fit well, and behavior imposed generates friction that wears down sympathy and patience.

Chief Justice Earl Warren's "all deliberate speed" gave an opportunity to involve teachers and parents in deliberation as to how to change to integrated schools. Autocratic administration was generally unable readily to adapt to or accept such procedure. The means of change were especially difficult because they ran counter to the prevailing mores of many communities and threatened the power of authorities in and out of school systems.

Rarely have modifications in the methods of teaching and alternatives to the methods of administering classes been considered. Rarely, too, "did desegregation occur under what was said by social scientists in 1954 [in their submission to the Supreme Court in the *Brown* case] to be conditions conductive [*sic*] to favorable outcomes for the children participating. It is surprising that outcomes have been favorable as often as they have." (Cook 1983)

In the summer 1980 edition of *Daedalus* there are three splendid articles by Atkin on "The Government in the Classroom," by Wood on "The Disassembling of American Education," and by Graham entitled "Whither Equality of Educational Opportunity?" Together they present an excellent, gloomy account of what has been occurring to American education and public school systems in the most recent decades. As in almost all discussions of precarious situations of our schools, of their seeming unawareness of change, and their sluggishness and ineptness in responding to change, these articles fail to sight even dimly the relationship of these factors to school administrative patterns or the hostility inherent in them. The very use of the word *even* in the quotation above—that teachers were "*even* resentful"—indicates the difficulty educators have in facing their hostility.

What has happened is that policy, substance, and methods of education have been determined with little participation in their formulation by parents, teachers, or students. The result has been a misfit of education to the situations in which parents, teachers, and students live and work. The courts and legislatures in attempting to cure constitutional defects have assumed that they could remedy failures or errors by imposing detailed procedures without participation of parents, teachers, and students at the points of application, the areas in which tensions develop.

Legislatures and courts by intervening have reduced the professional responsibility of teachers. They have declared schools failures and in effect put them in bankruptcy (in the case of the South Boston High School the Court actually placed the school in receivership) and told teachers and administrators how they must act, often in detail. They have been ordered to change their ways *instanter*. (In chapter 9 the process of change will be more fully discussed.)

Mind you, the move to *equal* education was proper. It was ethically essential as a means to improve our democracy. Young "niggers" had to be transformed to black children, as much children and Americans as any others. The "weaker" sex had to be acknowledged as just as strong as the male sex even if they could not usually swing a sledgehammer so well. The small country school and the urban ghetto school had to be assisted in supplying education equal to what better financed suburban schools offered. Handicapped children required recognition for abilities frequently ignored. These changes in attitudes or values have not been fully achieved, but they are more clearly in the view of educators than they had been.

What is troubling is the failure of courts and legislatures to understand how change can be most effectively implemented and their apparent refusal to recognize that the expense of putting into effect some commanded changes and newly recognized rights could not be met in most school districts except at the cost to other essential programs: class size, the arts, and other legitimate and educationally valuable activities. Federal funds, for example, supporting vocational education have been granted with specified proportions of vocational and general education, which has made flexibility impracticable.

Graham suggests that the strategy of the government has been based on two false premises: (a) that money can buy learning and (b) that by itself education will result in social and economic upward mobility. Both of these premises ignore the background, the hinterland of education, the limits of what money can buy, and the contradictions of social and economic power to a simplistic notion of upward mobility. Nevertheless, as Graham points out, these assumptions have been very generally accepted with the result that the schools have been made scapegoats where expectations of improvement have failed. (Graham 1980)

An interesting example of intervention by the courts in school administration is the case of *Goss v. Lopez* (1975). The Supreme Court held that a student suspended for up to ten days had to be given notice of charges and the opportunity to present his or her version of the incident "preferably prior to removal from school." While the court did not require hearings with counsel, confrontation, and cross-examination of witnesses, it nevertheless held that due process of law required that a student threatened with suspension be given an opportunity to defend himself or herself. A minority of the court dissented because it felt the decision required "indiscriminate reliance upon the judiciary, and the adversary process, as the means of resolving many of the most routine problems arising in the classroom." The minority opinion presents an arguable point of view against judicial intrusion in the classroom. However, the majority's holding demonstrates that the court felt the need to protect children against arbitrary authority, authority schools always assumed to be theirs to maintain discipline and decorum—or evade problems. In effect the Court was telling schools: if you want to teach democracy and justice you had better practice it.

Other Court decisions also have limited the powers of or enforced duties on schools.

For instance the Supreme Court held that school board rules requiring pregnant schoolteachers to take maternity leaves four or five months before an expected birth was arbitrary and denied due process of law, as did that portion of the rule making a teacher ineligible to return to school until her child was at least three months old. (*Cleveland Board of Education v. LaFleur* 1974)

The Supreme Court decided that a school system must provide English-language instructions to children of foreign ancestry who did not speak English, otherwise they would be denied a meaningful opportunity to participate in the public education program in violation of the Civil Rights Act. (*Lau v. Nichols* 1974)

There have been conflicting views by courts in their considerations of adoptions and removals of text and library books. When do the guaranties of the First Amendment and when do the freedom of educational authorities (teachers, librarians, school boards) prevail? (Estreicher 1980)

Legislation, state and federal rules, and court decisions frequently lack clarity. This has resulted in "the increasing role that lawyers and accountants are playing in program decisions." Neither teachers nor principals, but lawyers and accountants may "render final judgment on program plans" because it is they who have to defend against negative findings by government auditors. (Burnes 1978) Wood quotes a university president as saying, "It used to be that I asked our faculty if we ought to undertake a particular program. Now, I ask our lawyer first." (Wood 1980)

And so it would appear that courts and legislatures have had to intervene to assure equity and protect civil rights in schools. The courts often ineptly—as in many desegregation orders—and legislators frequently have inserted their own or their constituents' ideas of what and how children ought to be taught. In this network teachers and administrators feel increasingly powerless.

Legislatures, often for political considerations, can restrict schools or impose tasks on teachers beyond the time or expertise available. Courts in many areas must determine whether interventions to protect rights outbalance possible dislocations of accepted patterns based on custom and experience.

Principals and Other Supervisors

It has been said that the superintendent was "the benevolent ruler whose word was law." He has been described as being today's "harried, embattled figure of waning authority." (Tucker and Ziegler 1978) Educational professionals in state and federal governments, boards of education—with ears tuned to local elections or appointment—courts, and bargaining agreements with unions have reduced their powers, as has already been described to some extent. Although these changes in power structure tend to create less consistency and direction in administration, is it not a plus that the superintendent's words are no longer the law? Does it not offer to him and her the chance to gain power by involving teachers and principals intimately in decisions, an opportunity to lessen opposition and resistance?

From the findings and opinions of some of the authorities cited in this book, and from the author's personal experience, it would appear that the key person in creating a good atmosphere for teaching and learning is the principal. However hampered by autocratic school boards and superintendents, a self-assured principal has space for cooperative planning within the school and power to create an atmosphere of mutual trust and respect, and to reward initiative. Jungles have their open glades. There is always the opportunity in individual schools, therefore, to be better or worse than the environment of a school system as a whole. However much encouraged to use initiative, a principal personally insecure will deny teachers respect and freedom to improvise.

Because of insecurity at all lower levels of hierarchy, people will feel afraid of being told implicitly "toe the line or else." Supervisors share many of the anxieties of teachers. They, too, want the good opinion of others, especially those with power over them, and often they impose upon teachers unwanted, unrealistic, or irrelevant actions to enhance their own self-importance.

> Half the harm that is done in this world
>   Is due to people who want to feel important.
> They don't mean to do harm—but the harm does not
>   interest them.

(Eliot 1950)

When people feel themselves to be unimportant and deprived of a chance of self-affirmation, it affects their pride and dignity. Their "sense of ineffectiveness is bound to reawaken the earliest feelings of helplessness and weakness which [they] had as [children] with a corresponding tendency for . . . unexpressed, normal aggression to turn into hate and resentment. The self-employed craftsman with a sense of achievement is less likely to be hostile to his fellows than the organization man who feels himself to be nobody." (Storr 1968)

Chairman Mao declared:

> At the very highest level there is very little knowledge. They do not understand the opinion of the masses. . . . Their bureaucratic manner is immense. They beat their gongs to blaze the way. They cause people to become afraid just by looking at them. (Mao 1970)

Mao can certainly be considered an authority on authority. However, in his program to reduce the power of the bureaucracy, he created the terror of the Cultural Revolution which replaced the bureaucracy by an elite mob. For a hierarchy blind to the people, he substituted a vigilantism that saw everything and reacted negatively to every whisper. And while the Cultural Revolution lasted it impaired productivity—and crushed culture. Mao was correct. Bureaucrats frequently "cause people to be afraid just by looking at them." Fear may lead to anger and anger to incapacitation to accomplish what is wanted as, for example, the ability to achieve greater life space within a bureaucracy.

Favoritism and Merit Pay

Favoritism can pluck individuals from the field of nobodies. It leaves a field of the rejected and results in fierce jealousy and hostility. We are all acquainted with this phenomenon in sibling rivalries. A classic example is to be found in Genesis 37 where it is recounted that Jacob loved Joseph best of all his sons and made him a cloak of many colors. "And when his brothers saw that their father loved him more than any of his brothers, they hated him so that they could not speak a friendly word to him."

The hostility of teachers is aroused when colleagues are treated as favorites (just as children are when teachers show favoritism). Being able to play favorites gives special power to someone with higher status. It is, therefore, often beloved by administrators. For these reasons teachers and teacher organizations have generally opposed merit pay or bonuses for performance deemed by some supervisor to merit special reward. Admittedly, the line between favoritism and reward for work well done may be subjective both to the awarder and the awarded. That is why, when practicable, a group reward for group achievement may be more acceptable.

From time to time there has been justified public clamor about the competence of teachers and their teaching. At the same time it is recognized that such deficiencies are not universal. So in a culture in which to such a great extent dollars are the measure of virtue, there have been movements to give merit pay to those teachers who are especially good. There is always the suspicion that those selected for merit pay may not be chosen for merit but for friendships and political influence. It is also a question of the standards by which they are selected. Inevitably, jealousy—hostility—will be stimulated when such choices are made. Moreover, the choices of the individually meritorious would be unlikely to help the morale of other teachers who are passed over. Merit pay will not strengthen the joint efforts of a school to improve merit.

There are more creative choices than merit pay to individual teachers. Awards might instead go to schools that substantially improve their achievement. This would reward the entire instructional staff of such a school (or district). It would encourage the cooperation of teachers and principals.

They would compete as a group against other schools and school districts.

Another choice might be making an additional sum available to the budget of a school that showed a special merit. This additional sum could be used as the principal and faculty chose, to increase pay if they wished, to get better instructional material, etc., etc. And why not involve the students by making a grant to be used as they chose for the improvement of their school—for improving environmental conditions in the school, for example (but not for the football team or the cheerleaders)? The important thing in merit awards is to make them stimulating to the community of the school. To create improvement in a school (or school district) cooperatively will be more effective than competitively, and certainly there would be less chance of arousing jealous hostility.

The group approach to problem solving emphasizes an attitude of collaboration, a situation in which "What 'I' do means very little, but what 'we' do is very important." An example is profit sharing in industry under the Scanlon Plan. Under this plan, in the few places in which it has been used, committees of workers and management encourage suggestions that are then considered and screened at various levels by committees of management and union representatives. Management need not accept the final conclusions of the committees but it usually does. Savings are then put into a profit-sharing pot. Although profit is not the end result of educational institutions, the technique for encouraging, evaluating, and implementing suggestions is relevant. The success of the technique, of course, depends upon mutual faith and it encourages such faith. (Lesieur 1961)

The Louse in the Bonnet

Just as Robert Burns's lady with a louse in her bonnet did not have the gift of God to see herself as others saw her, so administrators, supervisors, and teachers appear to lack the same God-given gift. Those in authority perceive themselves as more kindly, more understanding, less autocratic, and more encouraging of two-way communication than their subordinates see them. (Throop 1972; Cullers et al. 1973; Foster 1976; Mangee 1976; and Likert and Likert 1976) Self-perception and status shade and color other perceptions.

In a study of secondary schools in Jamaica, even though no significant correlation was found between the appraisals by teachers and principals of their schools and the educational performance of the schools, there were considerable differences in the judgment of the behavior of the principals. There was an overestimate by principals of the amount of their support and friendliness, the confidence and trust of the teachers, and the freedom of teachers and students to talk to the principals, as well as the extent to which principals sought and used the ideas of others. The principals perceived the style of management of their schools to be on a higher level of consultativeness than the teachers. The students felt it to be far more competitive. (Horsman 1973)

In addition, age differences, experiences, and expectations result in different emphases on values and life goals. Baird in his study of *The Elite Schools* (1977), found, for example:

	Students	Teachers	Administrators
Standing up for your own rights	50%	22%	15%
Being independent and original	64%	54%	44%
Being nonconformist, different from other people	11%	1%	0%
Finding personal happiness	89%	78%	74%
Being of service to others	35%	69%	73%
Being independent of others	51%	40%	36%
Living my life in my own way without interference from others	45%	28%	33%
Changing the world for the better	54%	40%	40%

These considerable differences between students and adults in values and life goals exemplify Buber's "genesis" of youth.

Perhaps the reactions of teachers and especially supervisors may indicate that they have become jaded and cautious. Whatever expectations, creativity, and desire for freedom they may have had, the dynamic independence of their youth had retreated into the supportiveness of a protective shell. Sometimes folly of youth may congeal into a cautious folly that we often call maturity. As we grow older we like to call this common sense, but may it not really be a loss of creativity as a result of what Randall Jarrell called the "dailiness of life"? (1970) Therefore, generally, we can expect less creativity and daring; or, perhaps, if administrators were daring they never would have risen to be administrators.

Individualism and the apparent insistence of youth on personal gratification and expression are inherent in their "genesis," a living-out of teenagers' need for increased independence from their parents, a rebellious need to do "their own thing." This can become antisocial and destructive as it was during the 1960s. It can lead to use of alcohol and other drugs or vandalism, as symbols of do and dare. Social intervention is needed. But this cannot be achieved successfully through lectures; certainly it will not result from command by people with more authority, greater power, which will arouse counterattack. Social behavior can be learned by example or by experience, including, possibly, as Baird's statistics indicate, reading. That is why student participation in planning, in setting goals and standards of behavior, becomes essential, if we are to avoid student hostility, subservience, anarchy, or cynicism.

Furthermore, in the elite schools studied by Baird (1977), there is a different evaluation among students, teachers, and administrators of the influence of teachers. "Over half the administrators and over 40 percent of the teachers felt that teachers had an important influence on students' values, but only 21 percent of students felt this way. Some 45 percent of students but only 27 percent of teachers and 23 percent of administrators thought reading had an important role to play in students' values."

It is difficult to determine the effects of and receptivity to one's own teaching. The author once sent a questionnaire to former students in a course at a graduate school of public administration. The replies varied from "I'm sorry I took your course. It was a waste of time and money" to "As you know I hated the course and didn't finish it. Now I find it changed my life" to "Your course saved my head in our last revolution." Literally? We never know. We never know whether and where some idea or value correctly or incorrectly conceived will influence the life of a student. In this lies the challenge and the risk of teaching. And as administrators we rarely get adequate feedback of our influence or effect on others. We are usually afraid to receive such feedback.

We have noted how schools tend to suppress the originality and imagination of children. This in part may be a result of the teacher's own fear of taking the risk of originality or daring to be imaginative. As in the case of Louisa in *Hard Times* there may be a danger in a teacher's expressing "wonder" in the presence of authority. "Everything in life is based on daring," Buber said. "All the teacher must do is to point the direction. Then it is up to the pupil himself." (Hodes 1971) To this must be added supportiveness. May this not be an apt message to supervisors?

Teacher Organization

Teacher organizations have performed a necessary function by insisting on recognition of the rights of teachers and respect for them. Teachers for the most part have been underpaid. After twelve years of teaching they average nationwide only $17,000 a year and many may start at $12,000. Today schools have difficulty competing with industry for persons capable to teach science and mathematics. In a culture that relates status so largely to income, comparative undercompensation not only discourages many competent people from teaching but it also indicates disrespect for the teaching profession.

Teachers have been subjected to autocratic directions and penalties by boards of education and superintendents. Their contracts tended to be annual and for arbitrary reasons were frequently not renewed. Thirty years ago (and doubtless in some places today) it was a frequent practice to require teachers to contribute to the dominant local political party in order to retain their jobs. They had to "pay up or get out." They had no tenure, laws, or contracts to protect them. (Report of an Investigation, Mars Hill, North Carolina, 1951) Pregnant teachers were dismissed or forced to take long maternity leaves (not for their own health so much as because their students might inquire about the reproductive process). They were denied representation when presenting grievances or defending against charges. Except for college teachers, they still have little academic freedom.

Teaching is one of the most intense occupations, but teachers were, and often still are, required to perform many little school "housekeeping" tasks that reduce the time and energy they might spend with individual students.

The founders of the republic regarded education as essential to developing a body politic that could guarantee the future of the American Revolution and the new republic they established. (Cremin 1980) The concept of general public education was glorified but not the teachers who were expected to lead the next generation. Teachers through the centuries have not often been treated as the equals of the members of the community who employed them. Socrates was not the last teacher to be considered dangerous; but more often teachers appear to have been considered as persons who must exemplify the virtues of frontier simplicity and the most puritanical morality, or not be teachers.

As an illustration, in 1872 the rules for teachers of a school in St. Augustine, Florida, required a number of daily chores on the part of teachers. They had to fill lamps and clean the lamp chimneys, bring in a bucket of water and a scuttle of coal, prepare pens, whittling their nibs "to the individual taste of the pupils." While such chores are no longer appropriate, other chores are frequently imposed upon teachers, such as various policing and bookkeeping activities.

Among the rules of that school district were the following:

a. Men teachers may take one evening each week for court-
ing purposes, or two evenings a week if they go to church
regularly.
b. Women teachers who marry or engage in unseemly conduct will be dismissed.
c. Any teacher who smokes, uses liquor in any form, fre-
quents pool or public halls, or gets shaved in a barber
shop will give good reason to suspect his worth, intention, integrity and honesty.

The reward for teachers who performed their labor "faithfully
and without fault for five years" would be an increase of
twenty-five cents a week in pay "providing that the Board of
Education approves." While such regulations and "rewards"
have not continued far into this century (except in some cases
with respect to the dismissal of married teachers), the attitude
and spirit did not disappear. It was by organizing that teachers
were enabled to obtain fairer treatment, better compensation
and working conditions, and to insist that they be regarded as
free adults, no longer one rung above household servants. Organization has given teachers peer support and legitimized
counterattack against authority. Very good.

However, in the main, the stance of teacher organizations has
been confrontational, threatening to strike if their terms are not
accepted. If the laws provide no other way to achieve what they
deem justice, they may have no other option than to strike. But,
where the law forbids strikes by public employees and also
provides other means to adjust their claims, such as arbitration
(and especially when the courts have enjoined striking), the
strike is an act of force as illegal as mugging. (Of course when
teachers strike illegally it is a middle-class offense or crime and
not considered by the public as so serious as the lower-class
crime of mugging.) After returning to the classroom how can a
striker who defies the law teach respect for law—or expect his
or her authority in the classroom to be respected? Are students
not given contradictory cues to legitimate behavior and conflicting values of authority?

Confrontations, inevitably hostile, are rarely effective as means to resolve conflict. The power of one party may be so great as to overwhelm the other. But, in most cases, each party raises the ante and the tempo of hostility without favorable resolution. The alternative is to lower tension as by relieving anxieties, doubts, and threat to social power. If a situation or behavior is to be changed without overpowering an opponent, it is necessary to analyze the opposing forces: What are the points of agreement? What may be the commonality of goals? How can anxiety be relieved? What support is possible? (Lewin 1951)

When the forces of opposition are increased, the level of tension increases and this will result in fatigue, higher aggressiveness, greater emotionality, and a lower level of constructiveness. (Lewin 1951; Marrow 1969)

A settlement resulting from a strike, or a threat of one, may result in a sense of restitution of power or at least of achieving a more satisfactory balance; but the balance itself will be tainted with a sense of guilt, a repetition of the guilt children feel when by a tantrum they get their way against their parents. The school board or superintendent, the employers, will be left with a feeling of loss of power to the teachers. Here a win-lose solution leaves anger from a loss of power in defeat.

So even when one has enough power to overwhelm another, a residue of hostility remains as a psychological irredentism. This is less true when, as in law, or in arbitration, the adversaries present their cases before a neutral third party who, it is agreed, will determine the issues that are in conflict.

There are at times situations in which partisans are so fixed in their beliefs or programs that reduction of tension is or certainly appears to be impossible. I recall during the 1940s at the New York City Board of Education, rightist groups who appeared to be immune to fact, argument, or compromise would come before us. During the same period the Communist-dominated Teachers Union would demonstrate inside and outside of the boardroom with the intention of creating discord. To participate in confrontation with either group would have reinforced their goals to disrupt. It was better to publicize the facts through the press. The general public and the press, by supporting the board, eventually vitiated the efforts of these extremists. Such instances of attempts to use power to influence or intimidate school boards or teachers will occur from time to time. The temptation to meet such opposition by confronting it as the Precipitators desire should be avoided, for to do otherwise may quickly polarize the community.

In spite of tidbits of verbal, and frequently sanctimonious, assurances that they act for the good of the children, teachers' organizations have failed to use their powers and professional competences to make better learning situations. Although teachers' organizations have relieved teachers of some of the humiliating, hostility-producing practices of school systems, they have ignored the most important arouser of hostility: autocratic administration. This cannot be corrected by strikes or any other kind of confrontation.

Teachers' organizations have rarely, if ever, addressed themselves to the area of autocracy. In this they have behaved more like a hod-carriers' union than like organizations of professionals.

Although in some systems teachers have a voice in textbook selection and curriculum development, it is a rare school with a rare principal in which teachers have freedom to plan, to allocate budget funds, or attempt innovations. And teacher organizations have paid little attention to meeting the needs of teachers to participate in activities that may give them some sense of power in the practice of their profession.

In a study by the Rand Corporation of teacher contracts, almost all provisions were found to be for the protection of teachers and only one, establishment of instructional policy committees, concerned improvement of teacher participation in planning. Only 18 percent of contracts up to 1970 and 11 percent more between 1970 and 1975 contained a provision for participation in planning. (McDonnell and Pascal 1978) In other words, the contracts were defensive of teachers' rights but negative in their concern for teacher creativity and teachers' sense of power in the exercise of their profession.

Albert Shanker, the able president of the American Federation of Teachers, writing in *The New York Times* (September 28, 1980), protested a new procedure introduced by the Board of Education requiring high-school teachers to submit weekly "plan books" detailing their plans for the next week's lessons. This has long been the practice of elementary and junior high schools. After showing some of the absurdities of this "ritual" he wrote:

> Unfortunately, things are changing for the worse on this matter in the New York City schools. Instead of heading toward a more flexible approach in the elementary and junior high schools, the high schools are now moving into a ritualistic lock step with the others. The orders have come from above. . . . But so far all they have produced is widespread anger, ill-feeling and demoralization. Any educational innovation which is viewed as one more bureaucratic burden by the teachers who must implement it, which is imposed from above against their will, is bound to fail. . . . It tells us what the school system expects of teachers is not their cooperation to do the best possible job but blind obedience in carrying out rituals.

Shanker perceived the indignity and protested the imposition on the teachers. Although he speaks in vague terms of "a more flexible approach," he fails to consider the alternative that would give a sense of dignity to teachers by enabling them to share power in adopting new procedures.

Life can be conceived as a series of steps in apprenticeships, lifelong apprenticeships for teachers as well as students.

> . . . The apprenticeship for life may be ousted by a course of instruction set by syllabus. Ordeals that are initiations into successive stages of life may shrivel into examinations in arbitrarily selected bodies of cut-and-dried knowledge. (Toynbee 1963)

Teachers as well as their students—often without realizing it—will share ordeals and frustrations that shrivel such apprenticeship. Without a sense of apprenticeship, without some daring too, there is little likelihood of teachers or children—or any of us—achieving maturity.

In a land of so many schools there are, of course, exceptions in which teachers and administration have worked together to improve the system and its morale. For example, in Toledo, Ohio, a school district had been in considerable trouble. Schools were frequently closed, there was a teachers' strike, a shortage of revenue, and a failed bond issue. In 1981 the Toledo Federation of Teachers and the school system agreed on a method to solve the ever-present problem of incompetent teachers. The teachers' union selected some outstanding teachers who served three years as consulting teachers to train, help, and evaluate new teachers. They made recommendations to an Interim Review Board of nine members recommending which new teachers should be retained and which were not adequate to hold permanent positions. The Interim Review Board consisted of five teachers and four administrators and made the final recommendations to the superintendent of schools.

Experienced teachers also, if they were deemed to require help, were given it by outstanding teachers in the school and the principal. This help continued until either the teacher had improved to the point of being deemed successful, or if a decision was reached that the teacher did not improve sufficiently, a termination of employment was recommended.

Thus teachers gave help to their peers and participated in determining the adequacy of their peers. It eliminated a confrontation between administrators and teachers. It did not put the principal on trial as is so frequently the case where a principal recommends the termination of a teacher's employment. It improved the sense of power of the teachers and reduced their hostility to appraisal of their competence. It raised the morale of the teaching staff and the satisfaction of the community to the extent that the next bond issue was passed.

If hostility in schools is to be reduced it will be necessary to flatten power relationships and give members of lower strata of the hierarchy—teachers and students—a greater sense of worth. It will have to permit contenders to save face and to give them a sense that they have some power in the bureaucratic establishment or at least that they have a lesser sense of comparative deprivation and reduction of power. The next chapters will discuss some additional models that have been effective to this end.

8 Some Problems of Power and Class

A Sense of Power

Thus far consideration has been given to the nature of hostility, its arousal and effect on learning, children's potentials, the cultures they bring to school, some effects of the harassment of teachers, their bind in the educational hierarchy, and some incidences and results of the "battlefield" of the classroom. Some of the less effective ways schools have used to handle conflict have been mentioned. There has been discussion of a prevailing sense of insecurity, comparative deprivation, and lack of power to realize goals and satisfy needs resulting in a generalized grumble of dissatisfaction or overt hostile expressions of anger in schools.

We may now ask: Is this inevitable? Must confrontation be a pervasive posture of schools and school systems? Are there ways in which interactions that result in hostility can be reduced? There is considerable evidence from empirical research and experience in school administration that this is possible.

We can assume that most hostility whether repressed or overt is in the form of defensive aggression. (Fromm 1973) From a moral point of view defensive aggression may be more acceptable than vicious, destructive aggression. However, in terms of the effects on learning and teaching there may be little difference.

This is a generalization. There are often instances in which counteraggression may motivate a person to overcome and succeed, to exert his or her efforts to prove the original aggressor wrong. Einstein and Verdi may have been examples of this. Many high-school students have been motivated to take on extra work to enter college ahead of schedule or have left school to go to work to show themselves and their teachers that the latters' low judgments of them were wrong. But in general, defensive aggression brakes motivation and generates hostility that deflects from the task; it consumes energy and prevents the communication and empathy necessary to successful accomplishment. It defuses or destroys the creative capacity of a child, who must man or mend some bulwark to defend his or her ego, and inhibits the creative efforts of the teacher, hobbled by the bureaucratic system.

The use of power is the common means for conflict resolution. For example, we tend to use power or threaten the use of power in labor disputes, international disagreements, litigation, marital disputes, the suspension of difficult children, and the dismissal of nonconformist teachers. Not to use power in a confrontation may appear to be an admission of weakness. However, to use power in confrontations may dissipate it. For domination is the conquest of demoralized and truculent subordinates, of opponents, of a wasted land, and is unlikely to foster productivity, imagination, or inquiry.

Where conflict develops into a win-lose situation, which is common when it is based on authority-dependence, sizable distortions occur in the judgment and perception of opposing groups. (Likert 1961; Blake et al. 1964; Sherif 1956) This leads to error. What happens is that the opponents tend to have tunnel vision which limits the opportunity to see the problem in a broad frame of reference, in a field that is larger than the contenders. Both sides are likely to perceive the other as static and to depreciate and downgrade the work and capacities of their opposites and to blind themselves to unacceptable realities.

An example of this is how we Americans underrated the scientific and industrial capacities of the Soviet Union. I recall when we were staying at the home of a distinguished mathematician in India, the American consul general told us that the mathematician was suspected of being a Communist and that he would like our opinion of him. Our host, in the discussions we had with him, never took a Communist position or used any of the current Communist lingo. But he did state emphatically, as he had publicly, that we underrated the Soviet Union. A few months later the Soviets launched Sputnik.

The basic principle of conflict resolution is to determine first on how much the parties can agree, to what extent they have common goals, and then what are their respective anxieties or interests that have to be of concern. A precondition to conflict resolution, to the "reduction of defensive aggression, is the decrease of those realistic factors that mobilized it." (Fromm 1973; Lewin 1947) The ever-present question is: What is the conflict all about?

The question helps to establish the problem, to give a cue to what may be made more specific and manageable. Facing the question may avoid conflict. Ignoring the question may make confrontation inevitable. To ignore the field, the environment of the conflict makes its resolution impossible. This is as true of the questions teachers may wish to present to administrators as it is of those of children. Such freedom of communication requires that the questioner will not be blamed for inquiring or laughed at for asking. For "laughter can turn into a very cruel weapon, causing injury if it strikes a defenseless human being undeservedly: it is criminal to laugh at a child." (Lorenz 1963)

It has been assumed that the principal function of education has been to transmit knowledge and ethical values from generation to generation and that by assimilation of that knowledge and those values a tradition would be established that would make understanding, communication, and respect possible between generations. In large measure we adults still live on this assumption and expectation. However, the learning and skills of fathers and mothers can no longer be passed on to sons and daughters with assurance they will be appropriate.

Recent centuries, especially the present one, have increased the pace of change manyfold and made adaptation vastly more difficult. The sources and potentials of energy have multiplied, cybernetics have enlarged the capacity of the human brain, and electronics made possible new artifacts and increased the possibilities of their replication. The opportunities for the untutored ditchdigger, hodcarrier, seamstress, and loom tender have been reduced. And the robot impends over more manual and semiskilled occupations.

As we tend not to understand the language and rituals of foreign cultures, so also we tend not to comprehend the language and rituals of youth culture. To us this subculture is a strange mortar that can connect young people of varying backgrounds, but not us. This lack of understanding reinforces the normal variations in perception that result from different experiences and expectations. (Kilpatrick 1961)

The quotation from Aristophanes in chapter 1 indicates that this divergence between generations has a long history.

It has been said that young people have good reason to be materialistic and skeptical, even nihilistic. For "[c]ultural and political ideas today have a way of becoming obsolete surprisingly fast; indeed there are few of them on either side of any curtain that have not already done so. . . . " (Lorenz 1963)

The "angry young men" of our civilization, Lorenz goes on to say, "have a perfectly good right to be angry with the older generation . . . ," and "their mistrust of all ideals is largely due to the fact that there have been and still are so many artificially contrived pseudo-ideals 'on the market' calculated to arouse enthusiasm for demagogic purposes." We witness this in commercial advertising and in the made-up personalities of office seekers and officeholders. Probably of more importance to young people are the contradictions between the glorification of democracy and fair play in text and talk and their denial in life situations. As mentioned in chapter 7, the court had to assure students the right to a hearing before suspension (*Goss v. Lopez* 1975), some measure of self-defense against the power of authority.

And it took the judicial power to assure freedom of the

press for student off-campus publications. A court had to admonish school officials that they could not punish students for a pornographic publication published and distributed outside of the school grounds, because this would violate the First Amendment.

> The risk is simply too great that school officials will punish protected speech and thereby inhibit future expression. In addition to their vested interest and susceptibility to community pressure, they [school authorities] are generally unversed in difficult constitutional concepts such as libel and obscenity. Since superintendents and principals may act "arbitrarily, erratically, or unfairly," . . . the chill on expression is greatly exacerbated. (*Thomas v. Board of Education* 1979)

What commentaries these cases are on the attitude of school personnel, and on their lack of faith in democratic principles and fair play, on their view of authority over dependents.

Nowhere are young persons more often treated as part of a mass than in the usual conduct of their education, for all the noble talk about treating them as individuals. Nowhere are students more subject to authority and denied participation than in establishing curricula and the process of learning. Of course there must be some rudimentary common goals and skills. Of course teachers of large classes are physically and emotionally unable to help every student satisfy his or her own needs; but there are areas in which student participation in planning and implementation of studies can lessen the gap between teacher and student, reduce the student's sense of powerlessness and hostile reaction to schooling. Joint planning can create a bond based on greater mutual trust, if it is genuine, not pseudo as when the teacher uses authority to make every final decision. It would be idle to set forth a formula or formulas as to how such collaboration might be achieved. It would depend on will. It would depend on the personalities of teacher and students. It would differ from class to class, year to year as the mix of personalities changed.

Especially it would depend on the extent of the trust and confidence principals and teachers had in each other and in students—their subordinates, their dependents.

Through joint planning, even within the broad outlines of somewhat dated curricula, youth culture may enter the school legitimately and become a fulcrum for lifting wider learning. In this process, too, the teacher may also be a learner and the joint educational activity give to teacher and students mutual trust, a lack of which brings about William James's battlefield of the classroom with its inherent hostility.

In addition to youth culture, accepting the legitimacy of other subcultures can reduce hostility. A recognition of the history of blacks in America has indicated to black and white students the legitimacy of black culture and widened for teachers and students their understanding of American history. This recognition of black culture reduces the chances of misunderstanding and blacks' sense of powerlessness and humiliation.

Teachers' hostility also may be cultivated in a medium of powerlessness and anxiety. They, too, need to be integrated into planning and development of teaching methods, curricula, and goals. Union contracts may assure better pay, protection from arbitrary dismissal, and relief from menial duties. Such contracts should also help meet teachers' basic need for professional fulfillment; but they may even restrict such fulfillment, as when they prevent teachers from working voluntarily with children after school hours. Limitation of hours of service may be justified to prevent exploiting teachers, but would such a restriction be necessary if teachers felt themselves to be participatory partners in the educational enterprise rather than the recipients of orders in a bureaucracy in which initiative was discouraged and accountability equated to blame?

It would seem that the key to reducing fear of blame, hostility, and counteraggression in the classroom is one that will open the principal's and, perhaps more importantly, the superintendent's office to people on lower levels of the hierarchy, sometimes to children and parents, to participate in goal setting, planning, and evaluation. This is quite different from the trite boast that the door is always open—open to listening and reassurance but not joint participation.

Autocracy can determine the disposition of a problem, but it rarely solves problems because there are always ecological effects, each action and every person inducing other actions and involving responses from other persons. As already shown, persons in authority rarely see their acts as others do; and interactions of autocratic, coercive systems are far different from those of group collaborative systems.

It is inevitable that the person or persons with final responsibility should possess power. However, the question is, how is power to be utilized constructively, without hostile reverberations and destructive effects? *Encouraging cooperative activity at any level of a system serves to legitimize a distribution of power. This will go far in reducing hostility.*

Administration and management have traditionally been based on authority, on power over dependents, those who for one or another reason find it in their interest to submit. As historically the anointed kings claimed divine rights, the tendency has been for superordinates to presume a certain socially accepted sanctity to their powers. For their own sense of power autocracy appears to be in the bones of most administrators.

> *According to classical theories,* the gap is great and it is inevitable in organizations. Hierarchy is a part of the system of authority that is essential to the maintenance of order. . . . Not only do leaders have the legitimate right and the superior knowledge to justify their authority, according to classical views, but lower ranking members lack industriousness and must be supervised closely in a tight chain of command if they are to be induced to perform on the job. This places great responsibility on leaders and requires unusual talent. (Tannenbaum et al. 1974; italics added)

Experience as well as empirical research by psychologists have shown that the democratic leader is not devoid of power. (Lewin et al. 1939) The different styles of leadership in the

Lewin, Lippitt, and White experiment indicated that "the most critical aspects of leadership were the size and space of free movement allowed the children and whether the leader's power was used to support or obstruct" the children's behavior. The leader's use of power "basically affected the emotional climate of the group." (Cartwright 1966)

"Democratic leadership is not an absence of leadership. A do-nothing, let-the-boys-have-their-way type of leadership is *not* [a] natural extension [of] democratic leadership." To believe otherwise is to operate "under the false assumption that democracy is something between autocracy and anarchy." (Argyris 1957)

Diffusing a sense of power results in less hostility. A management, for example, that is more conscious of the human element in productivity will tend to have less absenteeism, less destruction of plant and matériel and less bitter labor relations. There will be less feeling by subordinates of subjugation and more loyalty to the organization because there will be more mutual respect. (Likert and Likert 1976) Deutsch (1973) has pointed out that a strategy of power and the tactics of coercion result in competitive relationships, whereas a strategy of mutual problem-solving through tactics of persuasion, openness and mutual support tend toward a cooperative orientation.

But the office of supervisor has authority, power, and it evokes defensiveness, defensive aggression, to maintain that power. Those who hold authority and power fear their diminishment, and struggle to maintain power by one or more political weapons: physical, economic, or psychological. (James Marshall 1969) The escaped slave who become priest of the Sanctuary of Diana at Nemi had constantly to be aware that another escaped slave might slay him and replace him in the priesthood. (Frazer 1923)

If I had a million dollars I'd be happy. Nonsense! If I were the top man or woman I'd have power to do what I wanted. Nonsense! There is always the fear of losing to someone or of something threatening, of opposition, of a social, political, or organizational earthquake or volcano. Power in itself does not eliminate hostility because its holders are rarely sure of its continuity and balance. That is why dictators fear democracy. That is the reason the "dictatorship of the proletariat" cannot trust the proletariat with power. This is the story of the Soviet Union and Hungary in 1956, of the Soviet Union and Czechoslovakia in 1968, and of the Polish Communist party and Solidarity in 1981.

It is a difficult lesson for supervisors to learn that shared authority may, nevertheless, leave with them a great power of leadership by which they can make the entire enterprise more effective.

How little participative management is understood by school administrators is illustrated in a book (*Profiles of the Administrative Team*) published in 1971 by the American Association of School Administrators, the largest national organization in that profession. There is a long discussion there of the position, duties, and opportunities of a director of human relations in a school system. It is somewhat difficult to determine whether this position is one of public relations or troubleshooting or training teachers or developing a curriculum in human relations. The very term human relations is left vague.

Where there are some statements in that book about the importance of teachers sharing in decision making, these are thrown out as pieties. The importance of participation, how there is to be participation, and the results or failure of participation by teachers in planning are ignored. Except in the most general terms "human relations" (however defined) are not integrated into the classroom environment, teaching, or learning. This publication illustrates the difficulty supervisors and administrators have in understanding the pressures of an autocratic hierarchy on teachers and students.

The quality of decision can be upgraded by leaders because their position, their authority, make it possible for them to protect persons with minority views as well as increasing their opportunity to guide the majority and dissenters in the process of problem solving. They have an adverse effect on the end product if they suppress minority views and use their position to promote their own views. (Maier 1967)

In addition to the importance of the motivational consequences of administrative style, "is the simple error proneness of the autocratic system . . . because the prerogative of deciding things unilaterally carries with it the privilege of being far more often wrong." (Bowers 1977)

Was the authority of Hitler, that resulted in the devastation of the German cities and the dismemberment of Germany, more effective than the often bungling democracies of England and the United States? Has the autocracy of Stalin and his successors been more effective in developing an adequate use of Russian natural and human resources and a more satisfactory life for the Russian people than the less autocratic, frequently contentious atmospheres of Western democracies? The Polish crisis of 1981 illustrates how autocratic error can defeat the very goals of an autocracy—dictatorship of the proletariat becoming dictatorship over the proletariat.

The Public's Role

In the background of a public school system is the public that can support or destroy its schools. It is not new to American schools that the expertise of educators will not be exalted or their values accepted by parents and taxpayers who are treated as outsiders. The community is informed in most instances through press, television, and radio. To assist in support of the schools the mass media have to be informed. Editors and reporters are eager for negative headlines that may bait their readers' hunger for an item that may reinforce their hostility toward their own schooling—or give them the self-satisfaction of saying that schools aren't what they used to be. The public has to be informed and involved in setting educational goals and values if education is to be more cooperative and democratic.

Parental interest in the education of their children is good for the children, good for the schools. It supports children's efforts to learn and tends to reduce conflict among the parents, the children, and the school. It can reduce the harmful effects of conflicting adult values discussed in chapter 3.

However, there are certain dangers in this too. Especially in small communities where parents and schools are so close together and principals and teachers can be buttonholed or called on the telephone at any time, parents frequently try to dominate schools, eliminate books, dictate teaching methods, and threaten school boards and school staffs. In one school system I have watched for many years superintendents rarely endure more than a few years, largely because of attacks by a few parents who influence some of the elected school-board members. Innovations and discipline are, in effect, made public issues and limit professional discretion.

Democracy requires that education be subject to the community as a whole and not merely in the hands of professionals. But as Charles A. Beard used to tell his classes at Columbia, "There is nothing that can destroy democracy more than too much democracy." The result is a frequent paradox between the ideal of democratic control of the schools of the community and incentive to professionals to be imaginative and effective, and be free of the dictates of popular moods. To maintain the degree of academic freedom the laws, the courts, and union contracts allow, school boards and teachers need to be supportive of each other in facing individual or community attempts to dictate to them.

Public, Private, and "Elite" Schools

A private or parochial school is not necessarily what is called an "elite" school. Nor are private, parochial, or elite schools necessarily better than public schools. Their quality depends to a considerable extent on the values of the qualifier. Some may be rated highly by educators and some third-rate.

A transaction relevant to the public schools that is impeding their development as schools for all the children has been the withdrawal of their children, to private and parochial schools, by much of the middle class. This has seriously hurt public education, especially when the remnant of students and parents are the deprived, the handicapped, or the victims of discrimination—as has happened in many school districts, particularly in inner cities. Private and parochial schools evade the problems of these important parts of the population. Troublesome children in particular are either denied admittance to the private and parochial schools or are passed back to the public schools when they create "trouble" or "problems."

Whatever the spoken or unspoken reasons may be for these withdrawals (whether for an allegedly better education, more opportunities for broader curricula, evasion of frequently unreasonable court-ordered travel time to and from schools, or just plain racial prejudice), an important result is the effect of leaving to public education so many of the educational problems. Those are frequently the hard-core problems of the "underclass," of the children of the poor, of youngsters with physical, social, economic, and psychological handicaps. When others are withdrawn it must leave the remnant with a sense of comparative deprivation and a sense of loss of social power. The public schools, then, more and more, may become wastelands of hostility. To teachers, this movement of children gives the message, we'll take the better, you take what's left over.

A result of the migration of middle-class children from public schools is that deficiencies of the public schools are forced to feed upon themselves. The withdrawing middle class and an aging population with no children become less ready to provide for public education budgets.

Hostility is not indigenous and limited to public schools. Consistently ignored is the aggression of students against students in boarding schools as well as off-campus aggression by students in strict private and parochial schools. The facile assumption that the conduct of youngsters in nonpublic schools is better than that in public schools is not necessarily so.

On a Manhattan street in New York City (about 1950) there

were a public and a parochial school. The windows of the public school were repeatedly broken; those of the parochial school were not. The immediate conclusion was that the parochial school students were better disciplined than those in the public school. However, a study of the situation showed that most of the windows were broken by the parochial students after school. It was less risky for them to counterattack against a school other than their own. (This is reported as an example of off-campus aggression not to be generalized as a finding that parochial schools develop more hostility than public schools. Both school systems do more than is healthful to society. Both systems also have schools with little hostility.)

The demand for tax credits to be granted to parents who pay for private education is another way of endangering support for public education. The theory is that people should not pay for the education of other people's children. On the other hand, would not people who send their children to the public schools be paying for the education of others' children in private schools by tax deductions or credits that increase their proportion of taxes? Such tax credits, of course, would be contrary to the whole philosophy of public education from Thomas Jefferson on. They would tend to create a two-caste system of education, a system for Myrdal's "underclass" and one for an upper class. How can one subscribe to this and yet, without a blush, teach democracy? One may wonder to what extent and in what proportion the middle class is committed to democracy.

The faults Coleman et al. (1982) found with the public school are not likely to be removed by further attrition through emigration of students to private schools. In spite of his contention that private schools are integrated, there can be no doubt that some are also established to avoid integration. (*Griffin v. School Board* 1964; *Bob Jones University v. U.S.* 1983)

A study of private and public high schools by the National Institute of Education interviewed high-school principals "in the neglected area of studies of private schools." (1981) Principals of public and private high schools reported, on the whole, satisfaction with their jobs. Private-school principals said that they had "less trouble on their campuses and more independence and authority within their schools, particularly in staff selection." They had more influence in management decisions and a greater sense of commitment. Parents had more say in public schools than in the private. Although the population of private schools was smaller and the students were largely of middle-class and upper-socioeconomic families, and though the private schools had the narrower mission to prepare their students for college "[e]ven by such a rough yardstick as National Merit Scholar winners . . . public schools make up eight of the ten top schools."

A study of elite schools reported: "Traditional schools were designed to prepare students for a niche in a society of conventional values. The need today is to make the school fit the needs of students ready to enter an unconventional—and unpredictable—society rather than to fit the student to the school." After discussing several possible reforms Baird proposes the involvement of students "in school decision making. *The idea is to have students experience democracy directly rather than as a theoretical proposition which was denied by their daily experiences.*" (Baird 1977; italics added)

Baird cites Gaines (1972) to the effect that:

> Academic excellence is the simplest and surely the most honest objective of the prestige schools. And in general they do provide a strong foundation in a selected set of disciplines. Their students do amass a considerable amount of factual knowledge; . . . Is any effort made to arouse a passion for truth or understanding? Is knowledge presented in a context of joy and wonder and excitement? Is that why all the way through school kids are constantly being classified by means of test scores, grades, rank in class, etc.? Personally, I no longer take very seriously our prestige schools' commitment to academic excellence (that is, as contributing to a richer, freer life, rather than merely as a step toward "making it" in the affluent society).

Baird is not in full agreement with Gaines on this because he says he does take a school's commitment to academic excel lence more seriously, "but, in agreement with him, I think that they have focused on an excessively narrow interpretation of intellectual tasks. In their search for excellence, many schools have raised the level of academic performance, believing that this practice would increase the quality and level of achievement of their students."

It cannot be reasonably argued that all private and parochial schools give a better education than all public schools. As has been noted above, private-school principals feel that they have more independence and authority than public-school principals. Is it not, perhaps, a fair hypothesis that where private schools do excel an important factor may be more democratic administration and classrooms, that is, where teachers are intimately involved in determining curriculum, teaching methods, discipline, and organization, and where students have less feelings of subordination? That is, *may not the quality of education be a function of the distribution of power?* Before accepting a conclusion that private schools necessarily give a better education than public, surely this is a hypothesis worthy of careful, empirical research.

Nonpublic schools have values in their greater freedom to experiment and as competitors to stimulate the public schools. They become dangerous to society, however, if they weaken the public schools or create on a large scale a caste system of education.

If the schools of a democracy become desperate enough they may find themselves compelled toward greater democracy. In this way there can be a reduction of confrontations, an increase in positive interaction between the various participants in school systems, and a better climate for teaching, learning, and creativity. To avoid defeatism, to gain achievement and the satisfaction of reaching educational goals they may be moved to a group-interactive, cooperative model of administration, a more democratic ethos. The storefront academies found success with dropouts and delinquents. Why can not the public schools be more effective with these same young people?

In the study of British schools already referred to, it was

concluded that the findings suggested that pupils were influenced not only by the manner in which they were treated as individuals but also that there was "a group influence resulting from the ethos of the school as a social institution." Consequently, it was said, there were strong implications that good behavior and attainments can be fostered by the schools even in a disadvantaged area. (Rutter et al. 1979)

This conforms to the finding by the Coleman study (1982) that those public schools in which there were greater academic demands and stronger discipline had the same high levels as private schools in achievement.

Each school has its own power system as a result of which hostility may be generated or reduced, and it does not matter whether these schools are called private, parochial, or elite.

Finally, for the most part, students go along and accept school's routines and disciplines "[a]s long as school is fun some of the time and rarely humiliating." But they still possess "the autonomous power not to." (Sizer 1984, pp. 140–211) They always retain the power to counterattack. It is well to remember that even the youngest have a power of their own on the classroom battlefield.

We have considered the scattering of power bases with their varying degrees of frustration and sense of lack of power. The resulting hostility is channeled into the struggles for power that are often devastating. Power struggles are not supportive of good teaching, learning conditions, or strong school systems: They reinforce the common bureaucratic pattern which Hannah Arendt called "control by NOBODY" (Arendt 1969), and emphasize a need to avoid blame rather than assume responsibility. Now let us look at the possibility of distributing power and reducing hostility.

9 Participation and Hostility Reduction

I was angry with my friend:
I told my wrath, my wrath did end.
I was angry with my foe:
I told it not, my wrath did grow.
  —William Blake, "A Poison Tree"

As in any other area of activity, schools and teachers must be responsible for their effectiveness. How much responsibility can they have and to whom are they fairly responsible if they "feel that their hands are tied by cook-book-type courses of study, line-item budgets, and short-range planning that deals exclusively with the process of education and not its products"? (Moeller and Mahan 1971)

Local conditions, the environment of each classroom, interaction of each teacher with each class cannot be generalized by lawmakers or officeholders in Washington or state capitals, or even by the offices of superintendents. It is only when teachers are encouraged and enabled to participate in decisions that to them are relevant to their jobs that they can fairly be held accountable, and this participation, of course, cannot be pro forma. Teachers cannot be invited to participate in planning if they are only encouraged to talk but the decision is left in the hands of a supervisor. They must be freely able to contribute their views and to set forth to a considerable degree standards on the basis of which they will be held accountable and by which they can hold themselves responsible. Examples of this, as well as of the uses of the faculty as a team to improve education and modify behavior, are well presented by Moeller and Mahan (1971).

Students may also have a place in planning and evaluation. "Students cannot be forced to learn. In fact, students have found many methods to avoid learning when they dislike the subject or the teacher." (Moeller and Mahan 1971) Students must be treated as partners in the learning process if they are not to be antagonists or subservient. Their enterprises, resistances, and questions can map the courses by which they can best pursue the course of study as well as indicate their individual styles of learning. "The student himself may be the greatest untapped resource in education." And the same may be said of teachers. Students and teachers are untapped resources largely capped by leadership they dislike or by dictates of immediate or distant authority.

In contrast, in a superb discussion of the English nursery and infant schools, the equivalent of our nursery schools and early childhood education, Lillian Weber (1971) compares them with our American schools. There was more openness in the English schools. They made greater use of the school environment. They had high standards which they tended to meet.

> For the most part, children in English infant schools functioned in an atmosphere where it was very easy to talk, *to ask questions*, to tell things about home to each other and to the headmistress and other adults in the school. Children functioned not as in a traditional "show and tell" program of limited talk, but as individuals, with individual concerns and with individual styles of talking. Even in whole-school activities, it was easy for children to offer their own comments on a point brought up by the headmistress. (Italics added)

The teachers there appear to have shared the attitude that it was important to accept and help *children's purposes.* The children's inquiries were respected. The child's interest in his and her environment cut across subject areas. This kind of scheduling not only supported a child's integration of experience but also sustained his and her involvement. The child's own experiences were more important than verbalism, than taking in what the teacher expounded. "The teacher's role in informal education could be summed up as *implementing and opening up a child's purposes.*" (Weber 1971)

The teachers in those English infant schools had a large part in planning. Planning was described as "child discovery . . . guided by the teacher." Thus, in effect, even the children of the infant schools participated with the teachers in planning.

Just as it has been found that the transition from our Head Start classes to our elementary schools has been difficult, so, too, the transition from the English infant school to the junior school has caused problems. The junior schools did not accept the child at his or her level of understanding but had its own fixed levels of achievement. Freedom of movement and interaction with adults and other children were limited. This would be harder on boys than girls because, as has been mentioned, boys tend to have a shorter attention span and require more physical movement.

There have been a number of suggestive reports on the use of groups of faculty, students, and, sometimes, parents in solving school problems and reducing tensions. (Berkovitz 1975)

One study found a feeling of aloneness on the part of students, teachers, and parents, and a sense of being at the mercy of outside influences too powerful for them to control. Teachers, students, and parents saw each other in stereotyped ways, perceived each other to be hostile, apathetic, or resistant. When brought into discussion groups, during 1969 and the early 1970s at the time when there was militant action on many campuses, "the open communication which resulted from the groups was effective in deterring destructive confrontations that might otherwise have occurred." Personal contact through discussion between teachers and students reduced confrontation. (Sarchet et al. 1975)

Discussion groups were a value to students because they gave them an opportunity for personal communication and because they saw themselves having "a place to have an effect" on the school. It was possible in some instances "to deal with some of the hostility between neighborhood gangs in the attendance area," when student leaders from several of the gangs were included in these discussions.

Another study showed a decrease in absenteeism as a result of counseling meetings. (Berkovitz 1975) Absenteeism is a symptom of hostility. One may wonder whether this was a "Hawthorne effect"—of feeling oneself important through participation; if so, it was all to the good.

Some Effects of Styles of Administration

Mary Parker Follett (1973) suggests that the job of the administrator is not how to get people to obey orders but rather to devise ways he or she can

> best *discover* the order integral to a particular situation. When that is found, the employee can issue it to the employer, as well as employer to employee. This often happens easily and naturally. My cook or my stenographer points out the law of the situation, and I, if I recognize it as such, accept it, even although it may reverse some "order" I have given.

She goes on to say that if orders were depersonalized there would be no "overbearing authority" or "laissez-aller" that arises from the fear of exercising authority which she described as "dangerous." The authority to be exercised is the authority, "the law of the situation."

Rensis Likert and his associates (1967) have made an intensive study of styles of administration in industry and schools. At the Institute of Social Research of the University of Michigan they obtained data from every hierarchical level in a number of industries. The study involved more than 20,000 managers and 200,000 nonsupervisory employees at a cost of $15 million.

They have constructed a continuum of systems. These systems extend from what they call System 1, the least effective in organizational functioning, to System 4, the most effective, which is based on group participation. The first three systems rely on person-to-person patterns of interaction. System 4 increases individual workers' motivation to contribute to the organization by giving them greater influence and participation in decision making and by affording them greater respect and appreciation of their skills and efforts.

System 1, which Likert calls "one-person—coercive" has, among others, the following characteristics: information flows downward and is received with great suspicion by subordinates to whom little information is provided. Decisions are made at the upper levels. Motivation is through monetary rewards and security—it depends on fears and threats, with occasional rewards. Employees are generally hostile and resistant to organizational goals. There is little trust in leadership. Subordinates do not feel free to discuss job-related problems with supervisors and goals are set by orders. There is no opportunity for discussion or objection.

System 2 is a person-to-person—competitive system. Communication is mostly downward and is viewed by subordinates with suspicion. There is little lateral communication between peers because there is great competition among them, each department head, for example, competing with others for the favor and support of his or her superior officers. The superior makes the decision, although occasionally consulting with the individual subordinates. Money and security, and rewards and punishments, are the primary motivational forces. There is limited confidence and trust between supervisors and subordinates, little influence of subordinates on goals or work methods. Goals are set by orders with little opportunity for comment by subordinates.

System 3 is also person-to-person, but consultative. The flow of information is up and down, the superior giving the most information and answering most questions. Downward communication is usually accepted; it may not be openly questioned by subordinates. The superior makes decisions, usually following discussion with subordinates. Motivation is achieved through financial security and recognition of a sense of personal worth. There are rewards and occasional punishments. There is considerable confidence between subordinates and superior and the former are able to discuss their work with the superior with some caution. The superior *usually* tries to get and use the ideas and comments of his or her subordinates. Goals are set after some consultation with individual subordinates.

System 4 is described as group-interaction—collaborative. In this situation information flows up, down, and laterally, that is, between those at the same level of organization. All relevant information is shared, and upward information is accurate and complete. Decisions are made by group participation usually with consensus, subordinates being almost always involved in decisions relating to their work. Motivation is achieved through security, money, and a sense of worth and achievement. There is high group-participation in setting goals, approving methods, and then appraising progress. There is a high level of confidence in leadership and trust between superior and subordinates. The latter feel free to discuss their jobs candidly with superiors. Superiors try to obtain and make constructive use of ideas and opinions of their subordinates. Goals are established with group participation.

The first and fourth systems—one-person—coercive and group-interaction—collaborative—rarely occur in pure form. Administration generally tends toward System 2, person-to-person competitive.

The Institute for Social Research conducted three field experiments in the management of companies in which the systems of management were moved toward System 4, the collaborative system. The evidence of these large field experiments indicated that company-labor relations and productivity were influenced by the management system.

Real and important differences continued to exist between the union and the company, but as the shift to-
wards System 4 progressed there was a great increase in
the capacity to attain acceptable solutions to difficult
problems. . . . Differences did not become formal grievances because they were solved at the point of disagreement. New contracts were negotiated without strikes and
without work stoppages. Both companies and union
members have derived substantial financial benefits from
the improved relationships.

In summary, they found where management systems tended
toward System 4, labor relations and productivity were the
best, and poorest where they tended toward System 1. (Likert
1967)

Another industrial study is relevant. The General Electric
Company's Personnel Research unit made a study of supervision some years ago. Among the findings was that in general
the foremen who were rated by their superiors as "most effective" claimed that they had significantly greater responsibility
than did those foremen who had been rated "least effective."
That is, "[T]he effective foreman assumes that he has full responsibility wherever there is any ambiguity about who is in
charge. The ineffective foreman assumes that someone else is
responsible." (Meyer 1972) In other words, the most effective
will take the risk of blame rather than be dependent on more
detailed instructions.

In this study G.E. also discovered that foremen rated poorer
would spend twice the time on production and related activities and approximately half of the time on personnel activities
compared with the more effective foremen. Both groups of foremen spent the same amount of time with problems of quality
control. However, the better foremen achieved better results in
quality. The foremen who were rated high by their superiors
and their subordinates tended to give general supervision,
whereas those rated low by their subordinates gave more detailed supervision. (Meyer 1972) The more effective foremen
did not breathe down the necks of their subordinates.

There are different variables in industrial and educational administration. School administration involves, among other things, socioeconomic status and home environment. The profit is easier to quantify in dollars than in learning. Nevertheless, a number of doctoral candidates have studied school administration within Likert's frame of reference and come to conclusions similar to those reached in the study of business enterprises. They concern the effectiveness of the several styles of management.

Administrative Style, Job Satisfaction, and Hostility

The school studies were made in various parts of the United States, in inner-city slums, and suburban and small-town schools. Some were of elementary schools, some of intermediate schools, others of high schools, and one was a study of a state education department. In every case the teachers in schools with administrative systems approaching group interactive, collaborative, were far more satisfied than those in schools approaching the one-person—coercive. (Prieto 1975; Shaw 1976; Morall 1974; Byrnes 1973; Reidy 1976; Smith 1975; Chung 1970; Carpenter 1970)

A study of administrators and professional employees of a state department of public education came to the same conclusion: "More supportive styles of supervision were found to be associated with higher levels of job satisfaction." (Thompson 1971)

Teachers in schools administered more toward the collaborative have been found to feel their needs were better satisfied than teachers in a more autocratic system. It also appeared that the former desired even greater involvement in decision making affecting their schools. (Wagstaff 1970)

In high schools and intermediate schools when teachers saw their department chairmen to be supportive in their leadership and as having high educational goals the lower was teacher absence rate. In other words, the better the leadership the lower the absenteeism. There was also a positive relationship between the way teachers appraised their department heads and their views of the leadership of their principals. (Likert and Likert 1976)

Administrative Style and Work Stoppages

As administrative practices approached System 4 and were collaborative, there was less tendency toward teachers' strikes and militancy. (Bernhardt 1972) Haynes (1972) studied ten schools that had had teachers' strikes for five or more days and ten in a nearby system that had never had teachers' strikes. He found that in those schools in which there had been no work stoppage, the respondents to his questionnaire (which included school board members, the superintendent, administrative assistants, principals, and teachers) felt themselves in varying degrees to be more involved in the decision-making process, and enjoyed greater confidence and trust in relations with each other than did those in the other schools. Subordinates and superordinates viewed communication, whether upward or downward, as being accurate. They had a generally better attitude about their school district as a place to work. The teachers in these nonstrike schools believed "to a significantly greater degree" than teachers in the other schools where there had been stoppages that overall the management in their district was more toward the participative group management style. The teachers themselves felt that they were more involved in decision making about school matters: the content of courses, instructional plans, teaching methods, and the behavior and activity of students. That is, they were more involved in decisions concerning *their own* work.

The relations between management systems and conflict were examined in thirty-three school districts. Where the management system was closer to the collaborative, System 4, there was less conflict in negotiating contracts. There was, however, no relationship between management system of a particular district and its grievance rates. (Langland 1978)

An urban school system that was undergoing racial realignments was temporarily closed because of student disruption. It had an administrative system close to System 1, that is, one-person coercive. A comparable high school in which the administration was closer to System 4 did not have strikes. Interestingly, students and teachers saw the differences between an autocratic-coercive and a collaborative group-interactive system of management, but principals did not. (Likert 1961)

In a study by Weeks (1978) of the relationship between conflict management by principals and the organizational climate in two large school districts, he found that the perception teachers had of the conflict management behavior of their principal was related to their perception of the organizational pattern of the school. The closer they perceived the organization to be collaborative the better they saw the principal's conflict management behavior. The larger the school the more teachers perceived the organization to be closer to the authoritarian, and the principals in larger schools reported their behavior to be more authoritarian than did principals in smaller schools.

In large organizations the distance between persons on the highest and lowest levels will necessarily be greater than in small organizations and the tendency toward impersonal autocratic administration will occur. The tendency toward autocracy could be mitigated by various techniques such as: distribution of responsibility to lower levels of organizations, creation of task forces composed of lower echelons, or the integration of levels of organization so that representatives of the next lower level would be on every planning or evaluating group. (Likert 1961)

Where there were high educational goals and adherence to high educational principles, teachers and students saw their school administration to be closer to the group interaction, collaborative style. In those schools teachers and students had more favorable attitudes toward their schools and were more highly motivated than in schools with other types of administration. (Caul 1976) Collaboration without high standards would, over time, become vitiating. At best it would amount to little more than a Kaffeeklatsch, or have the disabling results of permissiveness discussed in chapter 2.

Administrative Style and Student Achievement

There is substantial evidence that the morale of teachers or their favorable or unfavorable reactions to autocratic or collaborative systems of management carry over to the classroom. They affect the learning of children.

The New York State Pupil Evaluation Program was used to study the relationship of systems of management to school achievement scores. It was found that the closer the management of a school was to the collaborative, System 4, style, the greater the achievement score improved over several years. The evidence was stronger in the case of mathematics than for reading, but there was improvement in both areas. (Donlan 1978) There was a similar finding in a study by MacKillican (1975).

Belasco (1973) reports an experiment involving a project to introduce performance contracts into certain schools. In some of these schools subcommittees of the teacher organization and the parent-teacher association worked closely to prepare for the introduction of the project at the opening of the school year, and monthly meetings occurred thereafter. These, Belasco called high-involvement schools. Children studying in these high-involvement schools showed an average net gain in reading skill of 2.3 years of growth in the nine months of the project. This compared with an average of 1 year of growth by children not in the high-involvement project.

Children with teachers who had less dissatisfaction with their levels of participation in decision making acquired the highest growth in educational achievement. When teachers perceived themselves as having great autonomy, and teachers and parents felt less dissatisfied with their participation in decisions, there was higher growth in educational achievement by the students than when teachers and parents were less satisfied with their level of participation in decisions. Participation by teachers and parents in the planning and execution of this innovation was the central factor.

It was found in another study that where administrative systems were more collaborative as perceived by teachers and principals, students' achievement test scores were higher in relation to their intelligence scores than those of students where the administrative systems were more toward System 1, coercive. It is especially interesting that this relationship existed in inner-city schools, with a large proportion of blacks and children from lower socioeconomic levels, as well as in schools with fewer blacks and located in higher socioeconomic neighborhoods. (Gibson 1974) To the same effect are Cullers and others (1973) and Morall (1974). *This supports the idea that children may not be written off because of race or socioeconomic origin. The problem of educability may not be in them but in the atmosphere of their school.*

Under Title I of the National Education Act of 1965, schools with a low socioeconomic, deprived population receive financial help from the federal government. Under the title there is requirement that parents be brought into cooperation with the schools. For the most part there has been only pro forma compliance with this, the principal or teachers usually dominating parental participation. In an experiment (Schraft and Comer 1979 and 1980) the New Haven schools cooperating with the Yale University Child Study Center facilitated a cooperative enterprise between the teachers and parents of the Martin Luther King School, a kindergarten to fourth grade public school of 350 students in the black section of New Haven. The parents were encouraged to participate by gradual stages in the work and planning of the school. A few engaged in the program to begin with and more and more parents participated later on. "In 1969, King School ranked 32nd of the 33 New Haven elementary schools on standardized tests in reading and math. There was a high student and teacher absentee rate, much conflict between children, between children and staff, and between parents and the school."

By 1979 the population had become increasingly poor but, nevertheless, this school "had the highest standardized test scores of any Title I school in the city." It had the second-best student and staff attendance records in 1978 and 1979. This, we know, is an important indicator of satisfaction with the school. "While there are, of course, many factors which account for the change, the involvement of parents and subsequent fusion of the school and its community has been one of the most significant."

While this experiment definitely shows how school atmosphere can be improved with planned participation of parents, it should be noted that the process of university involvement is expensive and not available in most instances. The burden (and it would seem a proper burden) must be upon the individual schools themselves to adapt the relations of parents, teachers, and students to some similar pattern. This would need imaginative leadership in a school and, perhaps, courage to overcome bureaucratic resistance, conventional attitudes of most schools toward parents and of parents toward schools.

As the New Haven school experience indicates the introduction of change involving new persons—parents and community there—cannot be hurried. The ecological effects of changed relationships and changed personnel require respect. Those engaged in bringing about a change need also be wary of our American impatience that so often expects a successful end-result before the process has even got momentum.

Bringing About Change

So it is possible by a change in style of administration (management) to alter the atmosphere and morale of schools and improve the satisfaction and performance of teachers and their students. Why then is not what has been learned about different styles of administration more prevalent, more generally accepted and applied by schools? Because (1) this learning is not generally known; (2) its implications counter the habits and presumably the personalities of most administrators *and* their subordinates; and (3) change must be carefully, even solicitously, and cooperatively planned and introduced if anxiety and defensive hostility are not to be stimulated.

As style and organization of administration change, there will be distressing withdrawal symptoms, the extent and intensity of which will depend on the conviction and tact of higher ranks of authority and the extent to which subordinates participate in planning, experimenting in, and evaluating the change. Certainly it should be apparent that a more democratic system, a group interactive collaborative system, cannot be effectively put in operation by mandate, one-person coercive.

As anyone who has tried to reform a bureaucracy knows:

> [B]eyond a certain threshold of institutionalization, bureaucracy acquires a kind of functional autonomy. The sheer fact that a structure . . . has been in place "for a long time" becomes a sufficient reason to fight to preserve it. (Warwick 1975)

Furthermore, no organizational change of magnitude can "be accomplished by edict, especially if it is to last." This was illustrated in an attempt to reorganize the administrative area of the United States Department of State between 1965 and 1970. (Warwick 1975)

In 1965 William J. Crockett, deputy undersecretary of state for administration, presented a reorganization plan to some 450 managers and employees of the administrative area of the department. It was supposed to develop openness, participation, self-management, and decentralize responsibility. One hundred twenty-five positions were eliminated, 165 employees were transferred to other parts of the department, some of the relatively powerful unit managers were to be stripped of some of their powers. Most importantly, the number of bureaucratic strata was reduced by cutting out six layers of supervisors between Crockett and the operating managers.

There was fear and grumbling and complaint among those members who had had no part in the decisions that led to the new system. Crockett's objectives were in large measure defeated by the resistance of the staff. The plan was further undermined by outside pressures such as an unfriendly hearing before a committee of the House of Representatives.

Crockett left the service in 1967 and was succeeded by Idar Rimestad, who considered Crockett's system to be no good, and he so testified before a congressional appropriations committee. He proceeded to restore line supervisors to their old jobs. In 1969 Rimestad was appointed to an ambassadorial post.

He was succeeded by Undersecretary William Macomber, who was pressed by the White House to develop a reorganization program. Pressure to the same effect came from the Foreign Service Association, an organization of foreign service officers. Thus there were pressures from outside and inside the department. In 1970 Macomber spoke to a large meeting of staff of the Department of State. He warned that outside efforts were being made to reform the department and, as he believed those would be ineffective and uninformed, he asked the staff to undertake a self-study. Thirteen departmental task forces were created with rather loose guidelines. The task forces included some 250 career professionals of the State Department and 40 officers from other foreign affairs units. They were selected through a nomination system and volunteers. Each task force chose its own chairman and adopted its own meeting schedules.

A year later the reports of the task forces were combined and their recommendations for the most part were approved by the secretary of state. The very fact that the staff themselves had developed the reports prepared them to accept the implications of the reports' findings and changes required in values, attitudes, and practices. The staff had become emotionally involved. The changes were effective because they had resulted from simultaneous pressures, from the top, from inside the bureaucracy, and from the outside (the president and Congress). As Warwick demonstrates in his study of this change process in the Department of State:

> [O]ne simply cannot understand bureaucracy, or even explain much of an agency's organizational behavior, without considering such factors as congressional control, interest-group pressures, and alliances between agency officials and various external actors [sic]. Internal

factors are, of course, highly important, but they must be set in the larger context of agency-environment relations. (Warwick 1975)

In any school system or any individual school the success of an attempt to change procedures or policies will be greatly dependent on the total environment of the change. It must be acceptable to the top, to the teachers, and to the community, certainly to parents. In many instances the students, too, must understand change and find it acceptable.

Another instructive example of failure of change introduced by fiat occurred in the New York City school system in the 1940s. At that time many of the younger teachers and also alert administrators had been experimenting in the elementary schools in what was variously called "the activity program" or "progressive education." At the request of the Board of Education the state commissioner appraised this method of education and made a highly favorable report. The board then authorized the superintendent to introduce the new methods into the elementary schools.

The superintendent (a genial, kindly man—no autocrat by nature) thereupon ordered that they be used. Many teachers felt threatened by being required to teach in a new way. They were unprepared for this and became greatly upset and antagonistic. Were the old methods, their skills, and perhaps they themselves to be considered useless? This became tinder to groups that opposed modernizing instruction. They objected to the new program which they claimed on the one hand had been imported from Moscow and on the other said it must fail if used in New York because it had failed in Russia. The fire spread from the school system to the press, and there were letters and editorials and statements by "experts" of all kinds condemning the action of the board and the superintendent.

What these experiences emphasize is that people will resist change if they are not involved in planning for it, or if they do not understand it and its purpose, or if they feel threatened because they believe their previous skills and experiences are no longer wanted, that they have become perceived as dispensable.

In support of the advisability of participation by teachers in change is a study of the relationship of the management system of a school to its capacity for change. (Ladouceur 1973) This study concluded that the more a school was oriented toward participative group management the more it was capable of changing. Such management seemed to make the school better able to obtain and use new knowledge in coming to decisions. It also contributed to innovative behavior by teachers.

Another example of educational change mandated without guidelines and sensitivity to the disruption of existing patterns, and where a sense of threat is experienced, is the desegregation of schools ordered by the Supreme Court in *Brown v. The Board of Education* (1954). The decision required compliance "with all deliberate speed." Speed—not at all deliberate—was pressed by a mix of euphoria and political pressure. Counterpressures—anxiety and resistance to changes that countered established practice—bubbled up. The deliberation was in most instances scanty. Consequently the expectations for improved education for blacks and better integration and race relationships have generally not been achieved by court-imposed desegregation plans. "With regard to white attitudes toward blacks, 8 of 15 studies of desegregation show increased prejudice, 2 reported decreases and 5 yielded mixed or no-effect results. For 12 studies dealing with black attitudes toward whites, prejudice rose in 5, lowered in 6, and showed no change in 1." (Gump 1980) It was not the prescription in the *Brown* case but its administration that made it so difficult to digest.

Generally change is only successful when it has been gestated in planning. The nutrients in the gestation of change are ideas (imagination), reality (facts—anticipated interaction), time (work and patience), and humor. The history of desegregation of schools supports Lewin's force field theory (1947) to the effect that as you increase force to achieve an end you increase resistance. The feelings of threat and anxiety must be reduced and they can be reduced by sharing of power in bringing about the desired change. This process has been absent in most districts engaged in school desegregation. For the most part neither courts nor school officials appear to have been conscious of the process of change and the interactions and emotional experiences it involves.

The interaction of people involved in change may result in creativity or evolution. However, the result might be explosive. When more or less tight controls are relinquished, the initial response of subordinates may be aggression; or it may be apathy. What happens may be dependent on the culture of the organization, the community, or the nation in which the transactions occur.

In 1946, a year after the defeat of Hitler's Third Reich, I was at a meeting of German teachers and school administrators in the American Zone. The speaker was a distinguished American principal and he was talking about administrative and curricula problems in schools. When he had finished his talk he asked for questions. No one raised a hand. It became embarrassing. He probed for questions on specific topics. Still no response. Finally one German teacher got up and explained that for so many years they had not dared to ask questions it was difficult to do so. Fear of the *verboten* lingered.

I recall in a New York City school a new principal who convened his teachers every month to discuss school problems. For the first few months, when they discovered that they were really free to say what they wished, the meetings were largely expressions of grievances, including attacks on the administration of the school. This repressed hostility had to be vented, the counterattack released, before they were prepared to discuss constructively the school's problems as they saw them.

Each of us is continuously changing. As an old Adirondack guide used to say, "I'll recover, but I'll never be the same." Brodsky (1980) put it this way:

> But you never
> lie in the same bed twice,
> Not even if the chambermaid
> Forgets to change the sheets. . . .

In every social situation the mix of personalities varies from group to group, school to school, classroom to classroom. Changes of the inner and outer environments demand alteration in goals, reactions, and institutions. They necessitate, in the words of Lorenz (1963), "the periodic shedding of the shell" as by crustacea. The old may disintegrate, the new develop haphazardly or by the application of intelligent programming. In any case there is a period of uncertainty, of vulnerability to defensive reaction. The vulnerable aspects of the new plan need to be envisioned if it is to have a good fit to the changed situation. The clue to solution is in avoidance of coercion and confrontation and recognition that the new may threaten those who do not perceive that the old shell deprives them of freedom today or feel their security to be threatened. And that is why collaboration of all those affected, especially including those who disagree, is necessary in reaching a conclusion that can provide a new stable norm of organization and behavior. Participation in planning, implementing, and evaluating change relieves those involved of dread of their obsolescence.

We are reminded by Martin Buber that to solve the problems facing mankind today it is necessary to have some kind of cooperation. "The way to reach that point would be for the two opposing sides to talk as good merchants. Let them make a list, so to speak, of those interests which are common and those which are antagonistic." (Hodes 1971)

Timing also may be an important consideration in bringing about successful change. Time may be a fourth dimension of the ecology of effective administration. Bateson (1979) tells of a "quasi-scientific fable" to the effect that:

> [I]f you can get a frog to sit quietly in a saucepan of cold water, and if you then raise the temperature of the water very slowly and smoothly so that there is no moment *marked* to be the moment at which the frog should jump, he will never jump. He will get boiled.

The ecological laws apply to schools as well as to seas and mountains, deserts and jungles, the living and the lifeless.

In Deweyian terms this is *transactional*, ". . . in which all aspects of the process are contained, including purposes, past experience in the form of assumptions, and the future in the form of expectancies." According to Cantril (1950), "Each occasion of life can occur only through an environment; is imbued with some purpose; requires action of some kind, and the registration of the consequences of action. . . . All of these processes are interdependent. No one process could function without the other." (Kilpatrick 1961)

If there is not a great, rapid change in membership the culture of an institution tends to persist. After some deviation in interaction in the beginning, new members usually adapt to the customs and behavior patterns of the others. They tend toward cohesiveness, that is, assuming that they share the same goals. This is so whether the culture be authority-dependence or democratic-participative. A change to authoritarian culture can occur more easily than to a democratic. (Lewin et al. 1939) For the latter, patience may be needed. And acculturation to a democratic-participative organization is not likely to occur if leaders or members threaten, bully, or ridicule newcomers; for such conduct will arouse defensive hostility, alienation, and counterattack. Respect for deviants, for minorities, is the prerequisite to constructive consensus.

> The grave will render all alike.
> So, if only in our lifetime, let us be various
> (Brodsky 1980)

Some Essentials and Caveats

To move a school system or a school to a collaborative, participative, group-interactive style of management is not easy. Its success will depend on establishing sufficient faith and confidence that the necessary interaction can occur, and that there will be no intellectual or emotional sit-down by subordinates or brickbats from the outside.

Although they are not to be considered a list of "how-to-dos" the following are some essentials and caveats to the process:

The principal or superintendent, the authority, the power at the top, must be convinced that the collaborative, participative method of management is superior to others. There must be conviction at the top that the shared power remains power because it can improve performance and accomplish educational goals.

There will be difficulty in having principals or teachers assume responsibility if they have previously been schooled to cover up error or cover so much work in so much time and not to innovate.

Success is only possible if subordinates participate in the process of change. Parents, children, and the community may be proper participants at various levels of change so that they do not feel that the change has been imposed upon them.

Sudden creation of a democratic atmosphere where there has been little before is apt to result—often for a considerable period of time—in expressions of grievances before responsibility is assumed.

The persons in authority need to be frank and to state the problems they see or foresee, and restrain from the temptation to say what they hope will be the determination of their colleagues.

Disagreements and dissents should be respected, otherwise there will be a residue of resentment.

Where persons in authority feel that they cannot accept the suggestions of the others, there should be an explanation of their decisions without attribution of error or poor judgment by others. Otherwise the attempt to turn the administration into a collaborative style will fail and what will be accomplished will be at best a consultative style such as that in Likert's System 3.

Finally, it is better for leadership to be modest, to cloak its ego, to take the position that what *I* do means very little but what is important is what *we* do. This thought was well stated in a verse by Lao Tzu, in which he expressed the belief that the best leader was the one whom people scarcely knew existed, who talked little, and when he had fulfilled his work people would say "We did this ourselves."

It can be done. It has been done. Most of us have known at least one teacher who has given us the feeling that we shared, "We did it," not that he or she was *forced* to do everything. Many have experienced principals, superintendents, or other administrators who have been successful because they have interacted with others to bring about collaborative management.

Finally

Some of the phenomena of interaction, the transactions among and between students, parents, teachers, school administrators and the public have been considered here, particularly those relating to the handling and stimulation of hostility. The degree of hostility in such interactions has been shown to be of prime importance.

It would be unrealistic to set as a goal the elimination of all aggression and hostility from schools. There is no cure, of course, for hostility, no sure cure for social and economic conditions that affect schools. Repeatedly, there may be unstable teachers and sociopathic students. It is apparent, however, that much of the aggression and hostility can be reduced and must be for effective wholesome education. The style of administration and its effects on the school, the atmosphere it establishes, is most important to teaching and learning. And we have ample evidence that administrative style can reduce hostility in spite of social and economic problems. In the long run it will prove more effective for quality education than emphasis on "basics," for it affects the needs, the satisfactions, and the life space of the classroom.

The business of schools is children. It is to educate them so as to encourage their imaginations, inquisitiveness, and thus to develop their discrimination, judgment, and power to evaluate. Today, more than ever before, there is need to inquire, discriminate, and evaluate in order to recognize and understand the merchandising gloss put on products as well as officeholders who are sold by mass media, frequently doctored for the market like a car, a cleaning lotion, or a cathartic. If they are not to be the dupes of salesmen or demagogues, the graduates of our schools must have capacity to distinguish among the choices offered them. Hostility vitiates the power to evaluate, seeds counterattack, or leaves docility, dependence, and distrust.

We turn again to the statement of the Supreme Court:

> . . .Scholarship cannot flourish in an atmosphere of suspicion and distrust. Teachers and students must always remain free to inquire, to study and to evaluate. (*Sweezy v. New Hampshire* 1957)

This freedom cannot occur in an atmosphere of hostility and fear of blame, for they enslave. They hamper the imaginations and hobble the inquiring minds of teachers and students. They shrink the space of freedom craved as a basic human need.

There is a caveat about individual development. The current emphasis on "doing your own thing" without much consideration of the human environment can be disastrous. We are not independent and humans never have been. We are in social settings and always have been. Even when we ignore others we are interacting with them. I like to think of each individual as a soloist playing a concerto, that is, as important as the soloist may be, he or she is dependent upon and interacting with the orchestra. The role of a leader of a school, a classroom, or anywhere, like that of the conductor, is primarily to facilitate, to integrate, that interaction.

Bibliography

Arendt, Hannah. "Aggression." *New York Review of Books*, February 27, 1969.

Argyris, Chris. *Personality and Organization*. New York: Harper and Bros., 1957.

Asner, Edward. *Raised in Anger*. Public Broadcasting System program, January 11, 1979.

Aristophanes. *The Greek Way to Western Civilization*. Edited by Edith Hamilton. New York: Mentor, 1942.

Atkin, J. Myron. "The Government in the Classroom." *Daedalus*, Summer 1980.

Augustine, Saint. *The Confessions of Saint Augustine*. Translated by J. G. Pilkington. New York: Liveright, 1943.

Baird, Leonard L. *The Elite Schools*. Lexington, Mass.: Lexington Books, 1977.

Barker, R.; Dembo, T.; and Lewin, K. "Frustration and Regression: An Experiment With Young Children." *University of Iowa Studies in Child Welfare* 18, no. 1 (1941). See also Alfred J. Marrow. *The Practical Theorist*. New York: Basic Books, 1969.

Bateson, Gregory. *Mind and Nature—A Necessary Unity*. New York: E. P. Dutton, 1979.

Bazelon, David L. "Beyond Control of the Juvenile Court." National Council of Juvenile Court Judges, July 1970.

Belasco, J. A. "Educational Innovation: The Impact of Organizational and Community Variables on Performance Contract." *Management Science* 20 (1973).

Benne, Kenneth. *A Conception of Authority*. New York: Teachers College, Columbia University Press, 1943.

Berkovitz, Irving H., ed. *When Schools Care: Creative Use of Groups in Secondary Schools*. New York: Brunner/Mazel, 1975.

Bernhardt, R. G. *A Study of the Relationships Between Teachers' Attitudes Toward Militancy and Their Perceptions of Selected Organizational Characteristics of Their Schools*. Ph.D. diss., Syracuse University. Ann Arbor, Mich.: University Microfilms, No. 72-11, 825, 1972.

Bernstein, Jeremy. "Einstein and Bohr: A Debate." *The New Yorker*, April 16, 1966. From *Albert Einstein: Philosopher-Scientist*, edited by P. A. Schilpp. LaSalle, Ill.: Open Court, 1973.

Blake, R. R.; Shephard, H. A.; and Mouton, J. S. *Managing Intergroup Conflict in Industry*. Houston: Gulf Publishing, 1964.

Blake, William. "A Poison Tree." *Poems*. Viking Press, 1950.

Blumenthal, Monica D.; Kahn, Robert L.; Andrews, Frank M.; Head, Kendra B. *Justifying Violence: Attitudes of American Men*. Ann Arbor: Institute for Social Research, University of Michigan, 1972.

Board of Education, Island Trees Union Free School District v. Pico, 638 F.2d 404, 1980; aff'd. 457 U.S. 853, 1982.

Bob Jones University v. U.S., 103 S.Ct. 2017, 1983.

Bowers, David G. *Systems of Organization: Management of the Human Resource*. Ann Arbor: University of Michigan, 1977.

Boyer, Ernest L. *High School*. The Carnegie Foundation for the Advancement of Teaching. Harper & Row, 1983.

Boyle, R. P. "Functional Dilemmas in the Development of Learning." *Sociology of Education*, 1969.

Brehm, Jack W., and Cohen, Arthur R. *Explorations in Cognitive Dissonance*. New York: John Wiley & Sons, 1962.

Brodsky, Joseph. "Anno Domini," "Strophes." *A Part of Speech*. New York: Farrar, Straus & Giroux, 1980.

Brown v. Board of Education, 374 U.S. 483, 74 S.Ct. 686, 1954.

Bruner, Jerome S. "After John Dewey, What?" *Saturday Review*, June 17, 1961.

Burnes, Donald W. "A Case Study of Federal Involvement in Education," "Government in the Classroom—Dollars and Power in Education." *Academy of Political Science* 33, no. 2 (1978).

Byrnes, J. L. *A Study of Certain Relationships Among Perceived Supervisory Style, Participativeness, and Teacher Job Satisfaction*.

Ph.D. diss., Syracuse University. Ann Arbor, Mich.: University Microfilms, No. 73-7790, 1973.

Cantor, Nathaniel. *Dynamics of Learning.* 3d ed. East Aurora, N.Y.: Henry Stewart, 1956.

Cantril, Hadley. *The "Why" of Man's Experience.* New York: Macmillan, 1950.

Carnegie Quarterly 16, no. 4 (Fall 1968).

Carpenter, H. H. *The Relationship Between Certain Organizational Structure Factors and Perceived Needs Satisfaction of Classroom Teachers.* Ph.D. diss., University of Houston. Ann Arbor, Mich.: University Microfilms, No. 70-4491, 1970.

Cartwright, Dorwin, ed. *Studies in Social Power.* Ann Arbor: Research Center for Group Dynamics, Institute for Social Research, University of Michigan, 1959, 1966.

Cartwright, Dorwin, and Zander, Alvin. *Group Dynamics: Research and Theory.* 2d ed. Evanston, Ill.: Row, Peterson, 1960.

Caul, J. L. *A Comparative Study of Student, Teacher, and Principal Perceptions of Organizational Structure Between Middle Schools with High Levels and Those with Low Levels of Middle School Concept Implementation.* Ph.D. diss., Michigan State University. Ann Arbor, Mich.: University Microfilms, No. TSZ 76-5530, 1976.

Chang-Wou-Kein, [sic]. "Seven Paintings," II "His Song." *The Lost Flute, and Other Chinese Lyrics.* Translated by Gertrude Laughlin Joerissen. New York: The Elf, Publishers, 1929.

Chase, H. P., and Martin, H. "Undernutrition and Child Development." *New England J. Medicine* 282 (1970).

Chein, Isidor; Gerard, Donald L.; Lee, Robert S.; and Rosenfeld, Eva. *The Road to H: Narcotics, Delinquency and Social Policy.* New York: Basic Books, 1964.

Chung, K. S. *Teacher-Centered Management Style of Public School Principals and Job Satisfaction of Teachers.* ERIC Document Reproduction Service, #EDO42-259, 1970.

Clark, A. W., and van Sommers, P. "Contradictory Demands in Family Relations and Adjustment to School and Home." *Human Relations* 14, no. 2 (1961).

Clegg, A., and Megson, B. *Children in Distress.* Harmondsworth, England: Penguin Books, 1968.

Cleveland Board of Education v. LaFleur, 414 U.S. 632, 94 S.Ct. 791, 1974.

Cohen, Arthur R. "Situational Structure, Self-Esteem, and Threat-

Oriented Reactions to Power." In *Studies in Social Power*, edited by Dorwin Cartwright. Ann Arbor: University of Michigan, 1966.

Coleman, James S. "Equal Schools or Equal Students?" *The Public Interest* 4 (1966).

Coleman, James S.; Hoffer, Thomas; and Kilgore, Sally. *High School Achievement*. New York: Basic Books, 1982.

Connery, Robert H. Preface, "Government in the Classroom—Dollars and Power in Education." *Academy of Political Science* 33, no. 2 (1978).

Conrad, Joseph. *Heart of Darkness*. New York: Penguin Books, 1977.

Cook, Stuart W. "Cooperative Interaction in Multi-Ethnic Contexts." In *Groups in Contact: The Psychology of Desegregation*. Edited by N. H. Miller and M. Brewer. New York: Academic Press, 1983.

Cremin, Lawrence A. *American Education: The National Experience—1783–1876*. New York: Harper & Row, 1980.

Cullen, Countee. "Incident." *Caroling Dusk: An Anthology of Verse by Negro Poets*. Edited by Countee Cullen. New York: Harper & Row, 1927.

Cullers, B.; Hughes, C.; and McGreal, T. "Administrative Behavior and Student Dissatisfaction: A Possible Relationship." *Peabody Journal of Education*, January 1973.

Dayton, Delbert H. "Early Malnutrition and Human Development." *Children* 16, no. 6 (1969).

Deutsch, Morton. *The Resolution of Conflict: Constructive and Destructive Processes*. New Haven, Conn.: Yale University Press, 1973.

———. "Education and Distributive Justice: Some Reflections on Grading Systems." *American Psychologist* 14 (1979).

Dewey, John. *Liberalism and Social Action*. New York: G. P. Putnam, Capricorn Division, 1963. Also see Kenneth Benne. *A Conception of Authority*. New York: Teachers College, Columbia University Press, 1943.

Dickens, Charles. *Hard Times*. A Harper Classic. New York: Harper & Row, 1965.

Donaldson, Margaret. "The Mismatch Between School and Children's Minds." *Human Nature*, March 1979.

Donlan, Herbert K. "The Leader-Management System of the Elementary School Principal and Its Relation to Student Achievement." Ph.D. diss., New York University, 1978.

Dubos, Rene. *So Human an Animal*. New York: Scribner's, 1968.

Duncan, Otis Dudley. "Inheritance of Poverty or Inheritance of Race?"

In *On Understanding Poverty*, edited by Daniel P. Moynihan. New York: Basic Books, 1968.

Dweck, C. S., and Reppucci, N. D. "Learned Helplessness and Reinforcement Responsibility in Children." *J. Pers. Soc. Psychol.* 25 (1973): 109–16.

Eliot, T. S. *The Cocktail Party*. Act II. New York: Harcourt, Brace, 1950.

Elliot, Delbert S., and Voss, Harwin L. *Delinquency and Dropout*. Lexington, Mass.: D. C. Heath, 1974.

Erikson, E. H. *Childhood and Society*. 2d ed. New York: W. W. Norton, 1963.

Estreicher, Aleta G. "Schoolbooks, School Boards, and the Constitution." *Columbia Law Review* 80, no. 5 (1980).

Festinger, Leon. *A Theory of Cognitive Dissonance*. Evanston, Ill.: Row, Peterson, 1957.

Firestone, William A. "Participation and Influence in the Planning of Educational Change." *The Journal of Applied Behavioral Science* 13, no. 2 (1977).

Follett, Mary Parker, in Fox, E. M., and Urwick, L. *Dynamic Administration: The Collected Papers of Mary Parker Follett*. 2d ed. London: Pitman Publishing, 1973.

Foster, J. P. *Perceptions of Principals' Behavior as Rated by Teachers, Students, and Principals in the Junior High Schools in Chattanooga, Tennessee*. Ph.D. diss., Virginia Polytechnic Institute and State University. Ann Arbor, Mich.: University Microfilms, No. TSZ 76-23,216, 1976.

Francke, Linda Bird. *Growing up Divorced*. New York: Linden Press/Simon & Schuster, 1983.

Frazer, James. *The Golden Bough*. New York: Macmillan, 1923.

Freud, Sigmund. *Civilization and Its Discontents*. Edited and translated by James Strachey. New York: W. W. Norton, 1962.

Fromm, Erich. *Man for Himself: An Inquiry into the Psychology of Ethics*. New York: Rinehart, 1947.

———.*The Anatomy of Human Destructiveness*. New York: Holt, Rinehart and Winston, 1973.

Gaines, R. L. *The Finest Education Money Can Buy: A Concerned Look at America's Prestige Schools*. New York: Simon and Schuster, 1972. Quoted in Leonard L. Baird. *The Elite Schools*. Lexington, Mass.: Lexington Books, 1977.

Gibson, A. K. *The Achievement of Sixth Grade Students in a Mid-*

Western City. Ph.D. diss., University of Michigan. Ann Arbor, Mich.: University Microfilms, No. 74-15,729, 1974.

Glaser, Daniel. In Paul A. Strasburg. *Violent Delinquents.* New York: Monarch, 1978.

Gold, Martin. "Scholastic Experiences, Self-Esteem, and Delinquent Behavior: A Theory of Alternate Schools." *Crime and Delinquency,* July 1978.

Gold, Martin, and Mann, David W. "Alternative Schools for Troublesome Secondary Students." *The Urban Review* 14, no. 4, Agathon Press, Inc. (1982).

Goodlad, John I. *A Place Called School: Prospects for the Future.* New York: McGraw-Hill, 1983.

Gordon, W. *The Social System of the High School.* Glencoe, Ill.: Free Press, 1957.

Goss v. Lopez, 419 U.S. 565, 95 S.Ct. 729, 1975.

Graham, Patricia Albjerg. "Whither Equality of Educational Opportunity?" *Daedalus,* Summer 1980.

Griffin v. School Board, 377 U.S. 218, 84 S.Ct. 1226, 1964.

Gruenwald, P. "Fetal Growth." *Public Health Reports* 83 (1971).

Gump, Paul V. "The School as a Social Situation." *Annual Review of Psychology* 31 (1980).

Gurr, Ted Robert. *Why Men Rebel.* Princeton, N. J.: Princeton University Press, 1970.

Haynes, P. D. "A Comparison of Perceived Organizational Characteristics Between Selected Work Stoppage and Non-Work Stoppage School Districts in the State of Michigan." Ph.D. diss., Western Michigan University. Ann Arbor, Mich.: University Microfilms, No. 72-14,182, 1972.

Heal, K. H. "Misbehaviour Among School Children: The Role of the School in Strategies for Prevention." *Policy and Politics* 6(1978).

Hechinger, Fred M. *The New York Times,* April 8, 1980.

———. *Times,* November 4, 1980.

Hodes, Aubrey. *Martin Buber: An Intimate Portrait.* New York: Viking Press, 1971.

Holt, John. *How Children Fail.* Rev. ed. New York: Delacorte, 1982.

Hopkins, Gerard Manley. *A Selection of His Poems and Prose.* Edited by W. H. Gardner. New York: Penguin, 1963.

Horsman, Ormonde. "A Study of the Organizational Systems of Selected Jamaican Secondary High Schools." Ph.D. diss., University of the West Indies, 1973.

Horwitz, Murray. "Psychological Needs as a Function of Social Environments." In *The State of the Social Sciences,* edited by Leonard D. White. Chicago: University of Chicago Press, 1956.

Jackson, Philip W. "Secondary Schooling for Children of the Poor." *Daedalus,* Fall 1981.

Jacob, François. *The Logic of Life: A History of Heredity.* New York: Pantheon, 1973.

James, William. *Talks to Teachers on Psychology and to Students on Some of Life's Ideals.* New York: Henry Holt, 1899.

Jarrell, Randall. *The Voice That Is Great Within Us.* Edited by Hayden Carruth. New York: Bantam Books, 1970.

Jones, Richard M. *Fantasy and Feeling in Education.* New York: New York University Press, 1968.

Kallen, David J. "Nutrition and Society." *Journal of the American Medical Association* 215 (1971).

Kaufman, Bel. *Up the Down Staircase.* Englewood Cliffs, N.J.: Prentice-Hall, 1965.

Keyishian v. Board of Regents of U. of St. of N.Y., 385 U.S. 589, 87 S.Ct. 675, 1967.

Kilpatrick, Franklin P., ed. *Explorations in Transactional Psychology.* New York: New York University Press, 1961.

King, Martin Luther, Jr. *Where Do We Go from Here: Chaos or Community?* New York: Harper & Row, 1967.

Kunitz, Stanley. "A Choice of Weapons." *The Poems of Stanley Kunitz 1928–1978.* Boston: Atlantic, Little, Brown, 1979; also Hayden Carruth. *The Voice That Is Great Within Us.* New York: Bantam Books, 1970.

Ladouceur, J. "School Management Profile and Capacity for Change." Ph.D. diss., University of Toronto, 1973.

Langland, Alfred S. "A Study of the Relationship Between the Management Systems of Selected Oregon School Districts and Conflict." Ph.D. diss., University of Oregon, 1978.

Lao Tzu. *The Way of Life According to Lao Tzu.* Translated by Witter Bynner. New York: John Day, 1944.

Lau v. Nichols, 414 U.S. 563, 94 S.Ct. 786, 1974.

Lesieur, Frederick G., ed. *The Scanlon Plan . . . A Frontier in Labor-Management Cooperation.* The Technology Press of MIT and New York: John Wiley & Sons, 1961.

Lewin, Kurt. "Group Decision and Social Change." In *Readings in*

Social Psychology, edited by T. M. Newcome and E. L. Hartley. New York: Henry Holt, 1947.

————. *Field Theory in Social Science*. Edited by D. Cartwright. New York: Harper, 1951.

Lewin, K.; Lippitt, R.; and White, R. K. "Patterns of Aggressive Behavior in Experimentally Created 'Social Climates.'" *Journal of Social Psychology* 10 (1939): 271–99.

Lewis, Anthony. *The New York Times*, May 8, 1971.

Likert, Rensis. *New Ways of Managing Conflict*. New York: McGraw-Hill, 1961.

————. *The Human Organization: Its Management and Value*. New York: McGraw-Hill, 1967.

Likert, R., and Likert, J. G. *New Ways of Managing Conflict*. New York: McGraw-Hill, 1976.

Lippmann, Walter. *Public Opinion*. New York: Harcourt Brace, 1922.

Lorenz, Konrad. *On Aggression*. New York: Harcourt, Brace & World, 1963.

McDonnell, L. M., and Pascal, A. H. "Organized Teachers and Local Schools"; "Government in the Classroom—Dollars and Power in Education." *Academy of Political Science* 95, no. 2 (1978).

McGuinness, Diane. "How Schools Discriminate Against Boys." *Human Nature*, February 1979. See also D. McGuinness, and K. H. Pribram, "The Origins of Sensory Bias in the Development of Gender Differences in Perception and Cognition." In *Cognitive Growth and Development*, edited by M. Bortner. New York: Brunner/Mazel, 1979.

MacKillican, William S. "An Empirical Study of the Relationship Between School Management Patterns and the Change Toward Classroom Openness." Ph.D. diss., University of Ottawa, Canada, 1975.

Maier, N. R. F. "Assets and Liabilities in Group Problem Solving: The Need for an Integrative Function." *Psychological Review* 74 (1967): 239–49.

Mangee, C. *A Study of the Perceived Behaviors of Elementary School Principals and the Organizational Climate of Elementary Schools*. Ph.D. diss., University of Michigan. Ann Arbor, Mich.: University Microfilms, No. 76-9452, 1976.

Mao Tse-tung. "Speeches, Directions, and Letters of Mao Tse-tung." *The New York Times*, March 1, 1970.

Marrow, Alfred J. *The Practical Theorist: The Life and Work of Kurt Lewin.* New York: Basic Books, 1969.

Marshall, James. *Herald Tribune,* October 11, 1952.

————. *Swords and Symbols: The Technique of Sovereignty.* New York: Oxford University Press, 1939; New York: Funk & Wagnalls, 1969.

————. *Law and Psychology in Conflict.* Rev. ed. New York: Bobbs-Merrill (Michie), 1980.

Marshall, Lenore. "A Mother Thinks of Her Child." *Latest Will.* New York: W. W. Norton, 1969.

Maternal Nutrition and Family Planning in the Americas, Pan-American Health Organization, World Health Organization 11 (Scientific Pub. No. 204), 1970.

Mead, Margaret. *Blackberry Winter: My Earlier Years.* New York: Pocket Books, A Kangaroo Book, 1975.

Meier, Deborah, " 'Getting Tough' in the Schools—A Critique of the Conservative Prescription," *Dissent,* Winter 1984.

————. "Why Reading Tests Don't Test Reading." *Dissent,* Fall 1981.

Menninger, Karl. *Love Against Hate.* New York: Harcourt, Brace, 1942.

Meyer, Herbert H. "The Effective Supervisor: Some Surprising Findings." In *The Failure of Success,* edited by Alfred J. Marrow. New York: AMACOM, a division of American Management Association, Inc., 1972.

Meyers, M.; O'Brien, S.; Mabel, J.; and Stare, F. "A Nutritional Study of School Children in a Deprived Urban District [Roxbury, Boston]." *Journal of the American Dietetic Association,* 1968.

Misumi, Jyuji, ed. *Group Dynamics in Japan.* "Leadership" by Sanshiro Shirakashi. Fukuoka, Japan: The Japanese Group Dynamics Association, 1973.

Moeller, Gerald H., and Mahan, David J. *The Faculty Team: School Organization for Results.* Chicago: Science Research Associates, 1971.

Morall, H. H. *The Relationship Between Perceived Participation in School Management and Morale of Selected Black and Nonblack Teachers and Students in Volusia County, Florida, Senior High Schools.* Ph.D. diss., University of Miami. Ann Arbor, Mich.: University Microfilms, No. 74-23,405, 1974.

Murphy, Gardner. *Personality: A Biosocial Approach to Origins and Structure.* New York: Harper & Bros., 1947.

Myrdal, Gunnar. *Challenge to Affluence.* New York: Pantheon, 1963.

National Commission on Excellence in Education. *A Nation at Risk:*

The Imperative for Educational Reform. A Report to the Nation and the secretary of education, U.S. Department of Education. Washington, D.C.: National Commission on Excellence in Education, 1983.

National Institute of Education. "The Private High School Today." *Education USA*, March 30, 1981.

New Roles for Early Adolescents. National Commission on Resources for Youth, 1981.

Ortega y Gasset, José. *The Dehumanization of Art and Other Writings on Art and Culture*. New York: Doubleday, Anchor Books, 1956.

Price, Richard. "Observations on the Importance of the American Revolution, 1784." In *American Education: The National Experience, 1783–1876*, edited by Lawrence A. Cremin. Harper & Row, 1980.

Prieto, A. C. *An Investigation of the Relationship Between Participative Group Management in Elementary Schools and the Needs Satisfaction of Elementary Classroom Teachers*. Ph.D. diss., University of New Orleans. Ann Arbor, Mich.: University Microfilms, No. 75-21,917, 1975.

Profiles of the Administrative Team. Washington, D.C.: American Association of School Administrators, 1971.

Quarterly Review of Doublespeak 8, no. 3 (May 1982).

Ravitch, Diane, *The Troubled Crusade: American Education, 1945–1980*. New York: Basic Books, 1983.

Reidy, R. J., Jr. *A Comparative Analysis of Selected Public Elementary Community School Administrative Systems and Public Elementary Non-Community School Administrative Systems Using the Likert Administrative Systems Model*. Ph.D. diss., University of Connecticut. Ann Arbor, Mich.: University Microfilms, No. 76-7212, 1976.

Report of an Investigation, Mars Hill, North Carolina: A Case Involving the Coercion of Teachers Through Political Pressures. National Commission for the Defense of Democracy Through Education of the National Education Association of the United States, October 1951.

Restak, Richard M. *The Brain: The Last Frontier*. New York: Doubleday, 1979.

Rosenthal, R., and Jacobson, L. *Pygmalion in the Classroom*. New York: Holt, Rinehart and Winston, 1968.

Russell, Bertrand. *Mysticism and Logic*. New York: Doubleday, Anchor Books, 1957.

Rutter, Michael; Maughan, Barbara; Mortimore, Peter; Ouston, Janet;

with Alan Smith. *Fifteen Thousand Hours: Secondary Schools and Their Effects on Children*. Cambridge, Mass.: Harvard University Press, 1979.

Sagan, Carl. *The Dragons of Eden: Speculations on the Evolution of Human Intelligence*. New York: Random House, 1977.

Sarchet, Jeremy A.; Jines, Jack; and Haines, Gerald. "Fostering Hope and Responsibility in the High School by Student—Teacher—Administrator Discussion Groups." In *When Schools Care: Creative Use of Groups in Secondary Schools*, edited by Irving H. Berkovitz. New York: Brunner/Mazel, 1975.

Saul, Leon J. "The Individual's Adjustment to Society." *The Psychoanalytic Quarterly* 18, no. 2 (April 1949).

Schraft, Carol M., and Comer, James P. "Parent Participation and Urban Schools." *School Social Work Quarterly* 1, no. 4 (Winter 1979); New York: The Haworth Press, 1980.

Seaver, W. J. "Effects of Naturally Induced Teacher Expectancies." *Journal of Personality and Social Psychology* 28 (1973): 333–42.

Shanker, Albert. *The New York Times*, September 28, 1980.

Shaw, C. E. *A Comparative Analysis of Organizational Climate and Job Satisfaction at Selected Public and Catholic Secondary Schools in Connecticut*. Ph.D. diss., University of Connecticut. Ann Arbor, Mich.: University Microfilms, No. 76-14,296, 1976.

Sherif, Mustaphe. "Experiments on Group Conflict and Cooperation." *Scientific American*, November 1956.

Shiki. *Cherry Blossoms*. Japanese Haiku Series Three. New York: Peter Pauper Press, 1960.

Simmons, Lydia. "One Year Before the Class: The Diary of a High-School Teacher." *New York* magazine, December 7, 1981.

Simon, Herbert A. "The Corporation: Will It Be Managed by Machines?" In *Readings in Managerial Psychology*, edited by Harold J. Leavitt and Louis R. Pondy. Chicago: University of Chicago Press, 1964.

Simon, Herbert A. *The New Science of Management Decision*. The Ford Distinguished Lectures, vol. 3. New York: Harper & Bros., 1960.

Sizer, Theodore R. *Horace's Compromise: The Dilemma of the American High School*. Boston: Houghton Mifflin, 1984.

Smith, K.; Johnson, D. W.; and Johnson, R. T. "Can Conflict Be Constructive? Controversy Versus Concurrence Seeking in Learning Groups." *Journal of Educational Psychology* 73, no. 5 (1981): 651–63.

Smith, M. C. "The Relationship Between the Participative Management Style of Elementary School Principals as Perceived by Their Teachers and the Level of Teacher Morale." Ph.D. diss., University of Southern California, 1975.

Spock, Benjamin. *The Common Sense Book of Baby and Child Care.* 1st Ed. New York: Duell, Sloan & Pearce, 1945.

Spock, Benjamin. *Baby and Child Care.* 3d ed. New York: Meredith, 1968.

Stoddard, George D. *The Dual Progress Plan.* New York: Harper and Bros., 1961.

Storr, Anthony. *Human Aggression.* New York: Atheneum, 1968.

Stotland, Ezra. "Peer Groups and Reactions to Power Figures." In *Studies in Social Power,* edited by Dorwin Cartwright. Ann Arbor: University of Michigan, 1966.

Strasburg, Paul A. *Violent Delinquents.* A Report to the Ford Foundation from the Vera Institute of Justice. New York: Monarch, 1978.

Sugarman, B. "Involvement in Youth Culture, Academic Achievement and Conformity in School: An Empirical Study of London School Boys." *British Journal of Sociology,* 1967.

Sweezy v. New Hampshire, 354 U.S. 234, p. 250, 77 S.Ct. 1203, 1212, 1957.

Tannenbaum, Arnold S.; Kavcic, Bogdan; Rosner, Menachem; Vianello, Mino; Wieser, Georg. *Hierarchy in Organizations.* San Francisco: Jossey-Bass Publishers, 1974.

Thomas, Lewis. *The Medusa and the Snail: More Notes of a Biology Watcher.* New York: Bantam Books, 1979.

Thomas v. Board of Education, 607 Fed.2d 1043, 1979; Cert. denied, 100 S.Ct. 1034, 1980.

Thompson, D. E. "Favorable Self-Perception, Perceived Supervisory Style, and Job Satisfaction." *Journal of Applied Psychology* 55 (1971): 349–52.

Throop, R. K. *An Explanatory Survey of Teacher Job Satisfaction: A Path Analysis."* Ph.D. diss., Syracuse University. Ann Arbor, Mich.: University Microfilms, No. 72-6636, 1972.

Tinker v. Des Moines School District, 393 U.S. 503, 511, 1969.

Toynbee, Arnold J. "Education in the Perspective of History." In *The Teacher and the Taught,* edited by Ronald Gross. New York: Dell, 1963.

Trilling, Lionel. *Freud and the Crisis of Our Culture.* Boston: Beacon Press, 1955.

Tucker, Harvey J., and Zeigler, L. Harmon. "The Myth of Lay Control," "Government in the Classroom—Dollars and Power in Education." *Academy of Political Science* 33, no. 2 (1978).

Wagstaff, L. H. *The Relationship Between Administrative Systems and Interpersonal Needs of Teachers.* Ph.D. diss., University of Oklahoma. Ann Arbor, Mich.: University Microfilms, No. 70-2343, 1970.

Warwick, Donald P., in collaboration with Meade, Marvin, and Reed, Theodore. *A Theory of Public Bureaucracy: Politics, Personality and Organization in the State Department.* Cambridge, Mass.: Harvard University Press, 1975.

Watson, Andrew S. *Psychiatry for Lawyers.* New York: International Universities Press, 1968.

Watt, Kenneth E. F. "Man's Efficient Rush Toward Deadly Dullness." In *Ants, Indians, and Little Dinosaurs*, edited by Alan Ternes. New York: Charles Scribner's Sons, 1975.

Weber, Lillian. *The English Infant School and Informal Education.* Englewood Cliffs, N.J.: Prentice-Hall, 1971.

Weeks, James A. "The Relationship Between Conflict Management Behavior of Principals and Organizational Climate as Perceived by the Principals and Teachers in Selected Texas Public School Districts." Ph.D. diss., University of Houston, 1978.

Westermarck, E. *Ethical Relativity.* New York: Harcourt, Brace, 1932.

Winick, Myron. "Malnutrition and Brain Development." *The Journal of Pediatrics* 74, no. 5 (May 1969).

———. "Fetal Malnutrition." *Clinical Obstetrics and Gynecology* 13, no. 3 (September 1970).

Wood, Robert. "The Disassembling of American Education." *Daedalus*, Summer 1980.

Index

Acknowledgments

I acknowledge, with thanks, the help of my good friends Rensis and Jane Likert, who have inspired so many of us; to Keitha Capouya and Janice Thaddeus, who have been of great assistance in the preparation of the manuscript of this book; to Lillian Weber and Lawrence A. Cremin for their valuable suggestions; to Irving Howe, Joseph P. Lash and Trude Lash, and Robert Lekachman for reading the manuscript; and especially to Sarah Katz, whose patience and meticulousness have improved each version of the manuscript, who has puzzled with me over my handwriting, caught so many of my errors, and given me extra eyes.